3D FOLDED BLOCKS

 American Quilter's Society

P. O. Box 3290 • Paducah, KY 42002-3290
www.AmericanQuilter.com

Located in Paducah, Kentucky, the American Quilter's Society (AQS) is dedicated to promoting the accomplishments of today's quilters. Through its publications and events, AQS strives to honor today's quiltmakers and their work and to inspire future creativity and innovation in quiltmaking.

Executive Book Editor: Andi Milam Reynolds
Senior Editor: Linda Baxter Lasco
Graphic Design: Barry Buchanan
Cover Design: Michael Buckingham
Photography: Charles R. Lynch

Additional copies of this book may be ordered from the American Quilter's Society, PO Box 3290, Paducah, KY 42002-3290, or online at www.AmericanQuilter.com.

Library of Congress Cataloging-in-Publication Data

Baron, Geesje.
   3-D folded blocks / by Geesje Baron and Esther Vermeer.
      p. cm.
   ISBN 978-1-57432-664-2
   1. Patchwork. 2. Quilting. I. Vermeer, Esther. II. Title.
TT835.B2723 2010
746.46--dc22
                                                2009053846

Proudly printed and bound in the
United States of America

CONTENTS

DEDICATION

This book is dedicated to Geesje's sons, Jan, Hendrik, Ruurd, and Roelof; and Esther's daughters, Alida Simone and Corinna Sabrine.

ACKNOWLEDGMENTS

We, the authors, have been quilting together for about ten years now, and, for a while now, once a week or more, our husbands and children have watched us disappear into our studios together, giving us the time that we needed to brainstorm, quilt, and write this book. They have been encouraging and supportive whenever we needed them to be, and for that, we thank them all.

We thank our mothers, our grandmothers, aunts, and creative friends for surrounding us with fiber arts and friendship, including the Klokkequiltsters of Wijnewoude, The Netherlands; the Material Girls of St. Claude, Manitoba; and especially the Morning Glory Quilters of Carman, Manitoba, who have been big supporters and a source of encouragement for us, getting excited about this project with us every step of the way.

We thank Liesbeth van Hulsteijn (formerly Liesbeth Noordhuis) of Quiltservice, Frederiksoord, The Netherlands, whose booklet *Vouw Patchwork* inspired the workshops that led to the writing of this book.

We thank Myra Harder and Cori Derksen, whose experience and advice helped us get started.

We thank Andi Reynolds, our executive book editor, along with Linda Baxter Lasco and the entire team of editors and designers, who have been so supportive, patiently answering all of the questions first-time authors have.

And finally, we each would like to acknowledge the other, in that we are both so thankful to have our lives enriched by such a special friendship and to have someone with whom we can share our passion for quilting.

"We have different gifts, according to the grace given us." Romans 12:6 NIV

An Introduction to Folded Blocks Projects: Three-Block Sampler

This great fat-quarter project has been written as a tutorial for making folded blocks. Although Indiana Puzzle, Union Squares, and Dutch City are not all beginner level blocks, you'll use all twelve folding techniques to make them. If you decide to start with a different project, you can refer to this chapter for tips and tricks on cutting and construction.

Please be sure to refer to page 15 for additional tips and pages 90–92 for the folding methods in detail, and our Web site for more pictures and video demonstrations at www.3dfoldedblocks.com.

THREE-BLOCK SAMPLER, 9" x 22½", MADE BY THE AUTHORS. BLOCKS FROM TOP TO BOTTOM: UNION SQUARES, INDIANA PUZZLE, DUTCH CITY

Three-Block Sampler

MATERIALS

Fabric requirements (based on fabric at least 40" wide)

Amount	Color/Value	Block Color Code
6"	pale yellow (very light)	A
8"	yellow speckled (light)	B
8"	medium-blue batik (medium light)	C
8"	chartreuse batik (medium)	D
12"	royal purple (medium dark)	E
15"	chartreuse print (for borders and backing)	

Label your fabrics A to E.

Miscellaneous

Batting: 10" x 24"

CUTTING DIRECTIONS

Sashing, backing, sleeves, borders, and binding

From the royal purple cut:

6 sashing strips	1¼" x 4½"
6 sashing strips	1¼" x 6"
2 binding strips	1¼" x 24"
2 binding strips	1¼" x 10"

From the chartreuse print cut:

2 sashing strips	2" x 6"
2 border strips	2" x 20"
2 border strips	2" x 9"
2 split-sleeve strips	5" x 6"
1 backing	10" x 24"

Once these large components are cut, use the cutting charts and cut the block components from each fabric, sorting the pieces as you cut, each into their respective block pile, while their measurements are fresh in your mind. If you wait to sort until you are finished cutting, you may end up having to remeasure, especially on projects with more than three blocks.

CONSTRUCTION

All of the folding methods are summarized on pages 90–92.

When you are finished cutting, take the pile for each block and stack the pieces in the order they'll be sewn, with Step 1, the basic square, on the bottom.

Indiana Puzzle–easy

Step	Color	# of Pcs	Size	Folding Code
1	A	1	4½" x 4½"	-
2	D	4	3¼" x 4½"	D
3	C	4	3¼" x 3¼"	G-2
4	B	4	3¼" x 3¼"	A
5	C	4	1⅞" x 1⅞"	B

INDIANA PUZZLE FOLDING

Take the pile of Indiana Puzzle pieces and flip it upside down onto your ironing board so that the 4½" square is on top.

Step 1: Each block starts with a basic square of 4½", which includes a ¼" seam allowance. Place the basic square of color A right-side up on your ironing surface.

Step 2: Fold the four 3¼" x 4½" rectangles of color D in half lengthwise (**this is folding method D**). Press each fold firmly. Position the pieces on the basic square, one on each side, in a **counterclockwise** fashion, tucking the end of the last piece underneath the edge of the first piece and aligning the raw edges with the outside edge of the basic square.

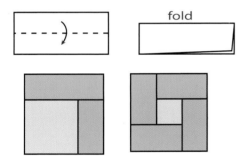

Step 3: Fold the four 3¼" squares of color C in half, then fold the left corner over, aligning the raw edges as shown (**this is folding method G-2**). Press and position them on the square. Raw edges to the outside.

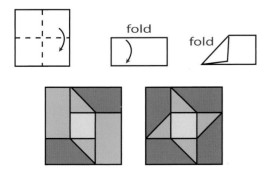

Step 4: Fold the four 3¼" squares of color B in half and in half again to form a quarter-size square with 2 finished (folded) sides (**this is folding method A**). Place each square on a corner, raw edges to the outside.

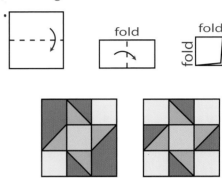

Step 5: Fold the four 1⅞" squares of color C once on the diagonal (**this is folding method B**). Place the resulting triangles in the corners, lining up the raw edges, to complete the block.

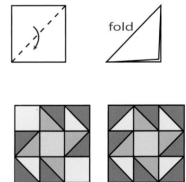

INDIANA PUZZLE ASSEMBLY

1. Carry the block to your sewing table. Remove one layer of the block at a time, and lay them on your table, one row for each step in the order you pull them off, leaving the basic block and the Step 2 pieces in place. Set your stitch length to about 10 stitches per inch.

Three-Block Sampler

2. With a ⅛" seam allowance, sew around your square to secure the rectangles, making sure that the raw edges line up. Remove the block from the machine, flip the block over, and trim off any excess fabric after sewing on each layer, taking care not to cut into the basic square. (See the tip on trimming, page 15.)

3. Position the Step 3 pieces counterclockwise on the block, so that the narrow points are tucked under. Each piece should meet the next so that the points of the star sit ¼" from the edge, and the inside corners of the Step 3 pieces meet the corners of the center square. Stitch around the block and trim. (See the tip on interior placement, page 15.)

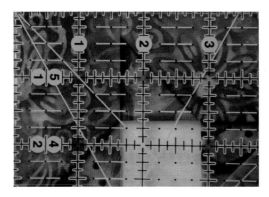

4. Place the Step 4 squares on each corner, raw edges to the outside. Looking from directly above the block, make sure that the inside corners of these squares line up with the corners of the light center square, and stitch.

5. Place the Step 5 triangles on each corner square, making sure that the corners of the color C triangles are ¼" from the raw edge. Stitch around to complete the block.

DUTCH CITY FOLDING

Dutch City–advanced

Step	Color	# of Pcs	Size	Folding Code
1	A	1	4½" x 4½"	-
2	C, D	2 ea	3¾" x 4½"	H
3	E	4	1⅝" x 3¾"	F
4	B	4	2⅛" x 3¾"	E
5	B	4	2⅛" x 3¾"	E
6	C	4	2⅛" x 2⅛"	B
7	A	4	1⅝" x 2⅛"	I

Take the pile of Dutch City pieces and flip it upside down onto your ironing board, so that the 4½" square is on top. Follow the tips given with the Indiana Puzzle instructions.

Step 1: Place the 4½" basic square right-side up on your work surface.

Step 2: Fold the four 3¾" x 4½" rectangles, 2 of each color, in half, then fold the 2 corners over (**this is folding method H**). Place the same colors opposite each other on the basic square as shown.

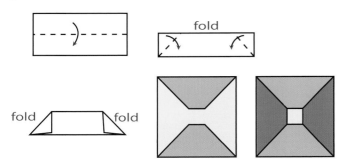

Step 3: Fold the 2 long edges of the four 1⅝" x 3¾" rectangles so that they meet in the center to make a long thin strip. Fold the strip in half across the width to form a rectangle with 3 finished sides (**this is folding method F**). Place them in the center of each side with the raw edge to the outside.

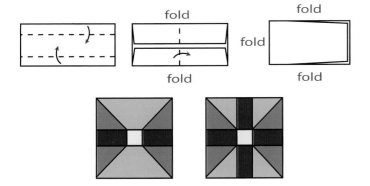

Steps 4 & 5: Fold eight 2⅛" x 3¾" rectangles in half lengthwise, then fold in half again across the width (**this is folding method E**). Place 4 of them, one on each corner with the raw edges to the outside. Then place the other 4, one on each corner in the opposite direction, as shown. (See the tip on sewing two layers at once, page 15.)

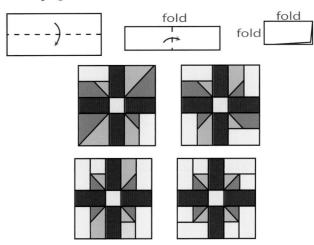

Step 6: Fold the four 2⅛" squares in half once on the diagonal (**this is folding method B**). Place each of these triangles on a corner.

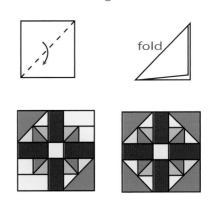

Three-Block Sampler

Step 7: Fold over ½" on the long edge of the four 1⅝" x 2⅛" rectangles. Fold both corners in so that the folded edge meets in the middle (**this is folding method I**). Place these triangles in the center on each side of the block.

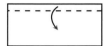 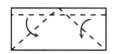 

DUTCH CITY ASSEMBLY

1. Carry the block to your sewing table. Remove one layer of the block at a time, and lay them on your table in rows, one row for each step in the order you pulled them off, leaving the basic block and the Step 2 pieces in place.

2. Position the 4 pieces so their edges butt up against each other. The inner and outer corners should line up so that the background fabric is only seen in the center (see the tip on pinning, page 15). Light pinning is recommended here. Sew around the block, beginning in the middle of one side, backstitching after each corner to ensure the pieces don't shift. Trim.

3. Position the 4 dark Step 3 rectangles on the block, making sure that the finished ends frame the center square, and stitch.

4. Position the 8 light rectangles around the square in a counterclockwise fashion, lining up the raw edges so that their finished ends butt up against the edges of the dark Step 3 rectangles. Stitch around the block. Trim where necessary.

5. Position the Step 6 triangles on the square, then position the Step 7 triangles on top. The inner edge of the Step 6 triangles should meet the corner of the inner square, and the points of the Step 7 triangles should line up with the edges of the Step 4 rectangles. Start stitching just before the corner on a Step 6 triangle, and sew around the square to complete the block, using your seam ripper to prevent shifting. Trim where necessary.

Union Squares–advanced

Step	Color	# of Pcs	Size	Folding Code
1	C	1	4½" x 4½"	-
2	B	4	3¼" x 4½"	D
3	D	4	3¼" x 3¼"	B
4	C	4	3¼" x 3¼"	A
5	B	4	2" x 2"	C
6	A	8	1½" x 2"	J
7	A	4	2" x 2"	A

UNION SQUARES FOLDING

Take the pile of Union Squares pieces and flip it upside down onto your ironing board so that the 4½" square is on top.

Step 1: Place the 4½" basic square right-side up on your work surface.

Step 2: Fold the four 3¼" x 4½" rectangles in half lengthwise (**this is folding method D**) and position them on the basic square, lining up the raw edges.

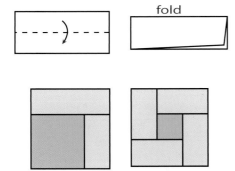

Step 3: Fold the four 3¼" squares in half once on the diagonal (**this is folding method B**) and place each triangle on a corner, lining up the raw edges.

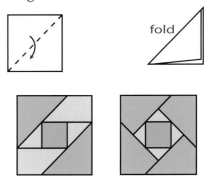

Step 4: Fold the four 3¼" squares in half and in half again to form a quarter-size square with 2 finished (folded) sides (**this is folding method A**). Position each square on a corner, lining up the raw edges.

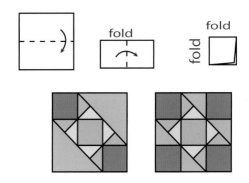

Step 5: Fold the four 2" squares in half on the diagonal and fold again on the diagonal to form a quarter-size triangle (**this is folding method C**). Position each triangle in the center of the sides of the block, lining up the raw edges.

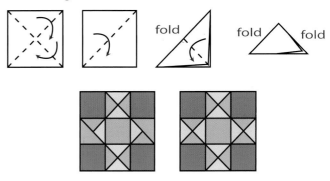

Three-Block Sampler

Step 6: Fold ½" over along one long edge of the eight 1½" x 2" rectangles. Fold both corners in so that the folded edge does not quite meet in the middle. Fold in half to form a quarter-size triangle with 2 finished edges with the folded edges on the inside (**this is folding method J**). Position the triangles so that the single-fold edge lines up with the edge of the center square.

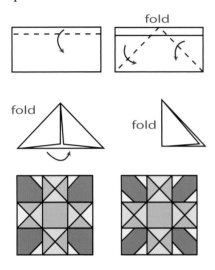

Step 7: Fold the four 2" squares in half and in half again to form a quarter-size square (**this is folding method A**). Place each square on a corner.

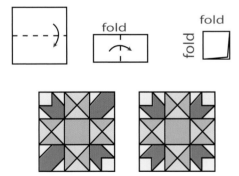

1. Carry the block to your sewing table. Remove one layer of the block at a time, and lay them on your table in rows in the order you pulled them off, leaving the basic block and the Step 2 rectangles in place.

2. Sew the 4 pieces to the basic square. Trim.

3. Position the four Step 3 triangles on the block in a counterclockwise fashion, making sure that their edges meet the corners of the center square, and stitch around the block. Trim.

4. Position the four Step 4 squares so that the single-fold edges are on the approach side of the presser foot, and the inner corners meet the corners of the center square. Stitch around the block. Trim.

5. Next, position and sew the three Step 5, 6, and 7 pieces all at once, one side at time, working counterclockwise. On each side of the block, the single-fold edge of the Step 7 corner squares should be on the approach side of the presser foot and the corners should line up with the point of the interior yellow triangle, as should the Step 5 and 6 triangles. The single-fold edges of the two Step 6 triangles should line up with the blue squares, while the Step 5 triangle tip should be centered. Work your way around the square to complete the block. Trim.

Quilt assembly

Sew the six 1¼" x 4½" royal purple sashing strips to the top and bottom of each block. Then sew the six 1¼" x 6" sashing strips to the sides of the blocks.

Referring to the instructions on adding borders to folded-block sashing (page 82), join the 3 blocks with the two 2" x 6" sashing strips.

Measure the length of the joined blocks along both long edges, find the average, and trim the two 2" x 20" border strips to that length. Add to the sides. Finally, sew the two 2" x 9" border strips to the top and bottom to complete the quilt top.

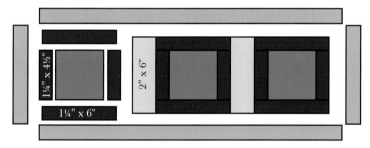

See the instructions on layering quilts with borders (page 82). Quilt as desired, add the split sleeve, and bind.

Review

At first you may need to refer to the master list of folds (pages 90–92) to interpret the short form of the folds, but very soon you will look at the shape you need, and you'll know exactly what to do.

Here are the short form folding instructions for these 3 blocks. This is the format you'll find for the remaining 67 blocks. Now that you've completed the tutorial, these should be easy to follow. You can always come back and review

the detailed instructions or refer to the master list of folding techniques (page 90–92) and tips (page 15), or find tips and additional photos on our Web site, www.3dfoldedblocks.com.

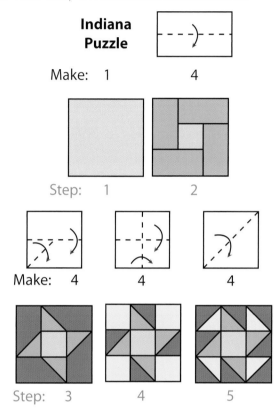

Three-Block Sampler

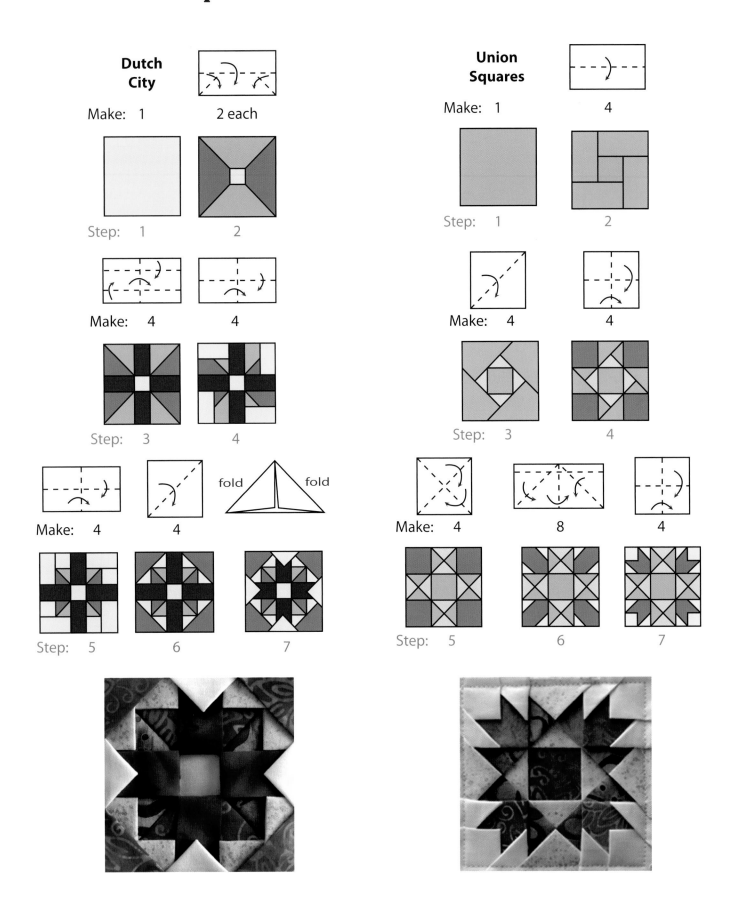

Dutch City

Make: 1   2 each

Step: 1   2

Make: 4   4

Step: 3   4

Make: 4   4   fold   fold

Step: 5   6   7

Union Squares

Make: 1   4

Step: 1   2

Make: 4   4

Step: 3   4

Make: 4   8   4

Step: 5   6   7

TIPS

Place pieces counterclockwise onto the block, so that as you sew around your block, the end of the previous piece covers the beginning of the next. This helps prevent shifting.

Pinning is not recommended, with one exception: when large folded edges need to meet tightly, then pin the center as shown in Dutch City, Step 2.

Having the interior points line up is more important than having raw edges line up. The **shapes made inside the block determine what the block will look like.** Keep in mind that the **layering diagrams do not show seam allowances.** The outer points should sit at least a ¼" from the edge.

If the raw edges don't line up after each step, trim them neatly, making sure not to cut into the Step 1 basic square. **Do not wait until the block is finished to trim**, especially for projects where blocks touch (for example, in STASHBUSTER). If the blocks are not trimmed, they won't sit square.

Use a seam ripper and your left fingertip to keep pieces in place as you sew. When needed, stop sewing before the needle reaches the next piece, lift the presser foot, secure the piece with the seam ripper's point, lower the foot, and continue sewing. This may also be needed when coming off a fold as well (especially on bias folds).

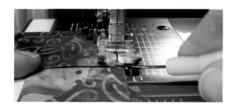

For **folding method J** (for example, on Union Squares, Step 6), make sure folded edges do not quite meet in the middle.

For blocks **where the Step 2 pieces do not cover the perimeter** of the basic square (for example, in Saint Gregory's Cross, page 45), position both the Step 2 and Step 3 pieces and sew them on at the same time, to avoid puckering in the basic square.

There are other times when **sewing two layers at the same time** is best or just faster (for example, Dutch City Steps 4 & 5, shown below, or Union Squares Steps 5, 6 & 7, shown at left).

Place the **double-folded pieces** (folding methods A, C, I & J, pages 90–92) so that when you are sewing them on, the single folds are on the approach side of the presser foot, since double folds tend to separate (for example in Indiana Puzzle, Step 4).

For **video tips and to ask questions**, please visit our Web site: www.3dfoldedblocks. com.

**Spring Flowers,
9" x 17½",
MADE BY THE
AUTHORS**

This pair of wallhangings began as an excuse to use something new in our studios and is a great beginner project. Neither of us spends much of our quilting time appliquéing, so feeling experimental, we decided to try out some oil sticks. These large oil paint crayons can be applied directly or brushed onto your fabric.

SPRING FLOWERS,
7" x 11½",
MADE BY THE
AUTHORS

Spring Flowers

Using a freezer-paper stencil, the effect of appliqué is created by applying the paint and, if desired, then stitching around the motif. You will need to wait 24 hours for your stencilled images to dry before you continue working with them and at least 3 days before heat-setting the paint. (Do not dry clean.) Choose one size or make them both!

MATERIALS

Fabric requirements for both quilts (based on fabric at least 40" wide)

Amount	Color	Block Color Code
8" x 30"	light background	
10" x 11"	medium background	
6" x 28"	brown	A
3" x 17"	pale green	B
3" x 17"	medium green	C
6" x 28"	light orange	D
5" x 28"	medium orange	E
½ yard	orange backing, binding, and split sleeve	

Note: If you plan to appliqué the leaves, you will need an extra 7" of medium green.

Additional supplies

Iridescent paint sticks: White, Leaf Green, Light Gold, and Copper
Stencil brushes
Parchment paper (to protect your iron when heat setting the paint)
Freezer paper for stencil template and paint palette
Batting: 8" x 12" and 10" x 19"

CUTTING DIRECTIONS

For the small quilt, cut:

1 backing	8" x 12"
2 split sleeve strips	4" x 6"
2 binding strips	1¼" x 8"
2 binding strips	1¼" x 12"

For the large quilt, cut:

1 backing	10" x 19"
2 split sleeve strips	5" x 6"
2 binding strips	1¼" x 10"
2 binding strips	1¼" x 19"

Cut the background pieces according to the cutting and placement diagram for the size(s) you're making.

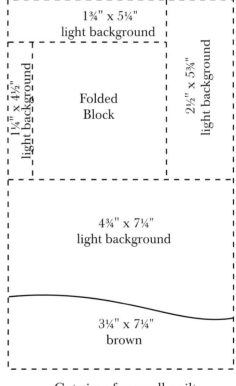

Cut sizes for small quilt

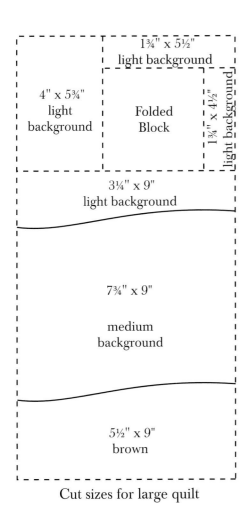

Cut sizes for large quilt

Folded block(s)

Follow the diagrams to make the Aunt Dinah block(s).

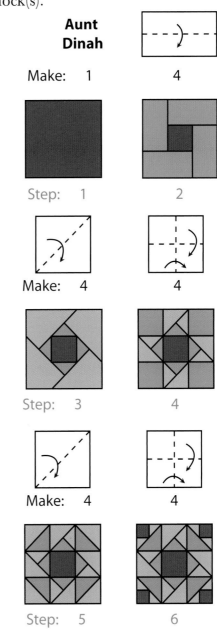

The folded block is the same size for both the large and small quilt. Cut the components for 1 or 2 blocks according to the Aunt Dinah cutting chart.

Aunt Dinah-intermediate

Step	Color	# of Pcs	Size	Folding Code
1	A	1	4½" x 4½"	-
2	D	4	3¼" x 4½"	D
3	B	4	3¼" x 3¼"	B
4	E	4	3¼" x 3¼"	A
5	B	4	1⅞" x 1⅞"	B
6	C	4	1⅞" x 1⅞"	A

Background

There's a fast and easy way to make this sort of background without templates.

Lay the brown background strip on the next background piece right-sides up with a 1½"–2" overlap, and cut a gentle curve through both pieces with your rotary cutter. Place right sides together, sew, and press the seam allowance toward the darker fabric. If you are not comfortable cutting freehand, lay a piece of contrasting yarn on your fabric in a gently curving shape and cut along that line.

Repeat the process for the second curved seam on the larger quilt.

Add the upper left background rectangle, sewing with a partial seam, stitching from the outside edge to ½" before the inside corner. Press the seam toward the larger piece. The folded block will be inserted later, since its thickness would interfere with painting.

Painting

Prepare your templates by tracing the patterns onto the dull side of the freezer paper. (See page 21.)

Working on the back of a cutting mat, cut out the vine with a utility or craft knife.

Iron the vine background shiny-side down onto the background fabric, positioning it so that there is about a half-inch of space between the leaves and the raw edges where the block will be inserted. Protect your work surface with plastic and tape the pieces down.

In the sample shown, the stem ends on the dark brown do not show up as well as on the lighter fabrics. By painting that area with white first, the colors painted on top will stand out better.

Remove a small piece of the skin from the white paint stick with a utility knife or by pinching off the skin with a bit of paper towel, and generously scribble some paint onto an 8" x 8" square of freezer or other non-absorbent paper. Using a large stencil brush, apply a solid coat of white to the darker brown fabric, being careful not to brush under your stencil.

Following the same procedure, brush on an almost solid layer of Leaf Green. Add Copper with the edge of the large brush along the wide parts on one side of the stem and on the circular tips to create shadows. Add some Light Gold highlights using a smaller stencil brush. Don't spend too much time near the seams, especially with the highlights, or you will draw attention to them.

The paint will be dry to the touch in 24 hours but wait for at least 3 days before heat setting. With the iron at the cotton setting (unless you are working with a fabric that requires a lower setting), position your background right-side down on a layer of parchment or brown craft paper to protect your ironing board from the paint. Press each section of the painted area for 10–15 seconds.

Preparing and inserting the block

Add the side and top background pieces onto the folded block, referring to the placement diagram (see page 18 or 19). Place the vertical edge of the block right sides together with the vertical edge of the upper left background rectangle and sew. Complete the partial seam and finish joining the block to the background.

Finishing

Layer, quilt, add the split sleeve, and bind.

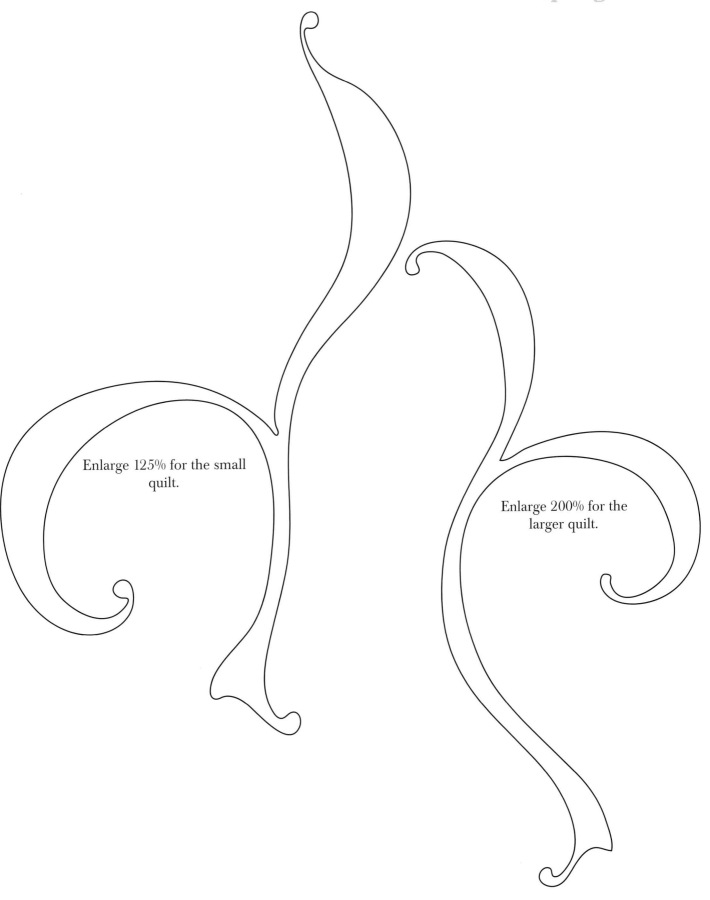

Enlarge 125% for the small
quilt.

Enlarge 200% for the
larger quilt.

NOTEBOOK COVER

NOTEBOOK COVER,
4½" x 6½",
MADE BY THE
AUTHORS

For this project we chose the Woodbox block because there is a window in the center of this frame-like block. You can fussy-cut your 4½" base square or even tuck a photo inside, mounted on a square of cardboard so that the subject is centered. This is a simple and quick project to make from a selection of fat quarters and scraps, perfect for a small gift.

MATERIALS

Fabric requirements (based on fabric at least 40" wide)

Amount	Color	Block Color Code
14" x 40"	main blue	
6" x 6"	focus fabric*	A
3" x 10"	light blue	B
3" x 10"	light blue 2	C
5" x 10"	dark blue	D
5" x 10"	dark blue 2	E
3" x 10"	pink	A

(for Step 4 only)

* For fussy-cutting, make sure that your motif will fit in the 1⅜" x 1⅜" center opening.

Miscellaneous

Batting: 7" x 14" and 6" x 6"

CUTTING DIRECTIONS

Cut the cover components from the main fabric:

2 strips	1¾" x 4½"	
1 rectangle	3⅝" x 7"	
1 rectangle	6" x 7"	
1 pocket	6" x 11"	
1 backing	7" x 14"	
1 binding strip	1¼" x 6½"	
1 binding strip	1¼" x 30"	

Cut the block components.

Woodbox-easy

Step	Color	# of Pcs	Size	Folding Code
1	A	1	4½" x 4½"	-
2	D, E	2 ea	3⅛" x 4½"	H
3	B, C	2 ea	1¾" x 4½"	D
4	A	4	1¾" x 1¾"	B

CONSTRUCTION ·

Woodbox folding

Follow the folding diagram to make the block.

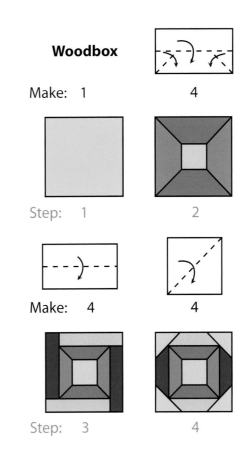

Cover assembly

If you have an image in the center window of your Woodbox block, make sure it is facing the right direction as you position and sew the outside cover strips and rectangles as shown.

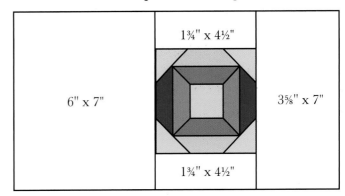

Notebook Cover

Place the Woodbox unit right-side down, lay the batting on top, and cut away a square of batting behind the block. Lay the backing (which forms the inside of the cover) over the batting. Pin or spray baste and quilt lightly around the block. Too much quilting will shrink the unit. Trim to measure 13" x 6½".

Fold the pocket rectangle in half right-sides together, sew a seam along one of the two open sides, perpendicular to the fold, and turn inside out. Place the 6" x 6" batting in between the 2 layers and quilt lightly. Trim the raw edges to make a 5½" x 5½" square.

Place the Woodbox unit right-side down (making sure the top of the center image is pointing away from you). Pin the quilted pocket to the lower right-hand corner of the inside of the cover, lining up the raw edges.

Baste the 2 outside edges inside the ¼" seam allowance. Topstitch the pocket in place along the left side. Add a second line of stitching 1" to the right of the topstitching for a penholder.

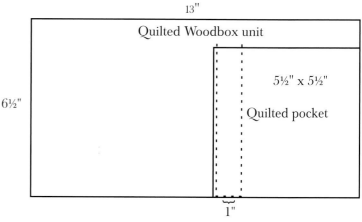

With the Woodbox unit outer-side up, bind the right edge of the cover. With the inner-side up, fold over the bound edge to the inside about 3" to form an interior side pocket. Pin the top and bottom edges. Secure the side pocket by binding around the remaining 3 sides of the cover.

Insert a pen and small pad of paper.

Garden Gate

Garden Gate, 14" x 14½", made by the authors

This is a quick and easy project. The Poppy and Duck Tracks blocks each have only four steps and, without large outer borders, the project requires no quilting. Once the blocks are done, you join them with sashing, make your quilt sandwich, add a sleeve, bind it, and it's done!

Garden Gate

The best thing about this Nine-Patch is that when you decide you want something new on the wall, you can repurpose this little wallhanging into a front pocket for a shopping bag (page 32).

MATERIALS

Fabric requirements (based on fabric at least 40" wide)

Amount	Color	Block Color Code
9"	white	A
19"	green	B
10"	yellow	C
30"*	black	D

* includes backing, sleeve, and binding

Miscellaneous

Batting: 17" x 17"

CUTTING DIRECTIONS

Cut the borders, binding, and split sleeve pieces.

From the black, cut:

24 sashing strips	1⅛" by 4½"	
1 binding strip	2¼" by 64" (piece as necessary)	
2 sleeves	6" x 7½"	
1 backing	17" x 17"	

From the yellow, cut:

16	cornerstones	1⅛" x 1⅛"

Cut the components for 5 Poppy and 4 Duck Tracks blocks (multiply the number of pieces for the total number of components to cut).

CONSTRUCTION

Folded blocks

Follow the folding diagrams to make 5 Poppy and 4 Duck Tracks blocks.

Duck Tracks-easy

Step	Color	# of Pcs	Size	Folding Code
1	A	1	4½" x 4½"	-
2	D	4	3⅞" x 3⅞"	B
3	B	4	3¼" x 3¼"	C
4	C	4	1¾" x 1¾"	A

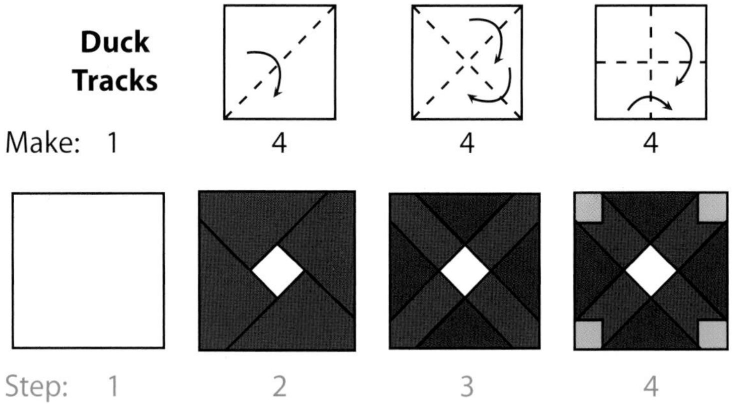

Duck Tracks

Make: 1   4   4   4

Step: 1   2   3   4

Poppy-easy

Step	Color	# of Pcs	Size	Folding Code
1	D	1	4½" x 4½"	-
2	B	4	3¼" x 4½"	D
3	C	4	3¼" x 3¼"	A
4	A	8	1⅞" x 1⅞"	C

Poppy

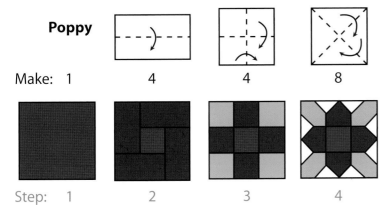

Make: 1   4   4   8

Step: 1   2   3   4

ASSEMBLY

Join the blocks, sashing strips, and cornerstones as shown.

Add the batting, backing, and sleeves and bind.

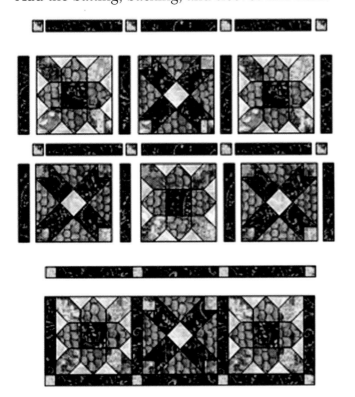

BLOCK PROGRESSION:
BREEZE CATCHER AND TRINKET BOX

TRINKET BOX, 5" x 5" x 5",
MADE BY THE AUTHORS

Building folded blocks from the bottom up, you might have noticed that at several steps along the way, the blocks are already appealing. These projects display that special feature, showing the progression of a block from the basic square to completion, although either project can also be made using a selection of your favorite blocks instead.

BREEZE CATCHER, 6" x 42",
MADE BY THE AUTHORS

The trinket box works with six-step blocks, but you can choose any block for the breeze catcher, guided by how long you want it to be.

MATERIALS

Fabric requirements (based on fabric at least 40" wide)

For the BREEZE CATCHER (BC):

Amount	Color	Block Color Code
21"	medium blue	A
4"	pale green	B
19"*	dark red	C
11"	dark blue	D
5"	dark green	E

For the TRINKET BOX (TB):

Amount	Color	Block Color Code
14"	tan	A
10"	green-brown	B
8"	blue-green	C
21"*	red-brown	D
6"	red	E

*Includes extra for binding

Miscellaneous

Batting for both: (2) 10" x 15" plus scraps for TRINKET BOX strips
5 beads for BREEZE CATCHER: ½" oblong or any shape with a vertical hole

CUTTING DIRECTIONS

Cut the following, using the project color codes.

BC Color	TB Color	Pieces to cut
A	A	(2) 10" x 15"pieces*
D	B	5 sets of Step 2 squares
A	D	5 sets of Step 2 squares
C	C	4 sets of Step 3 squares
E	E	3 sets of Step 4 squares
B	A	2 sets of Step 5 squares
A	A	1 set of Step 6 squares

*To be quilted before cutting into Step 1 basic squares

Breeze Catcher and Trinket Box
Sandhills-intermediate

Step	BC Color	TB Color	# of Pcs	Size	Folding Code
1	A	A	1	4½" x 4½"	-
2	A	B	2	4½" x 4½"	C
	D	D	2	4½" x 4½"	C
3	C	C	4	3¼" x 3¼"	B
4	E	E	4	3¼" x 3¼"	A
5	B	A	8	1⅞" x 1⅞"	C
6	A	A	4	1⅞" x 1⅞"	A

Cut the remaining components as follows:

For the BREEZE CATCHER, from color C, cut:
12   1¼" x 4½"
12   1¼" x 5½"
And for the sleeve, from color A, cut:
1   4½" square

For the TRINKET BOX, from color B, cut:
8   1¼" x 4½"
8   1¼" x 5½"
4   1⅝" x 5½"
4   1⅝" x 6½"
From batting scraps, cut:
4   ½" x 4½" strips
4   ½" x 5½" strips

CONSTRUCTION

Folded blocks

You need 6 densely quilted basic squares for your blocks. The dense quilting is not only decorative but it also provides stiffness to the squares that will prevent the breeze catcher from sagging or the trinket box collapsing. Inserting a layer of stiff interfacing will do the job, too.

Layer the 10" x 15" batting between two 10" x 15" pieces of your basic square fabric. Pin baste and quilt it densely in a pattern of your choice.

Breeze Catcher and Trinket Box

For the BREEZE CATCHER, we chose a quilting pattern called Garlic, also known as Teardrops. Surprisingly, this pattern is a lot easier than basic stippling, since you can work out of tight spaces and move across your work simply by echoing the shapes you are stitching around. We chose a zigzag sort of meander for the TRINKET BOX.

Cut each quilted piece into 6 squares 4½" x 4½". Mark the good side of your quilting with a pin. You'll build your blocks on the opposite side.

Set aside one quilted basic square (the best one, since this one won't be covered at all) and lay out the remaining 5 in a row, good-side down. Proceed to position the folded and pressed components on each block, taking each consecutive block one step further, so that your row looks like the folding diagram.

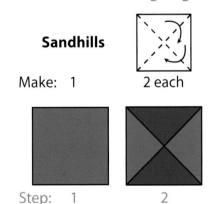

Sandhills

Make: 1   2 each

Step: 1   2

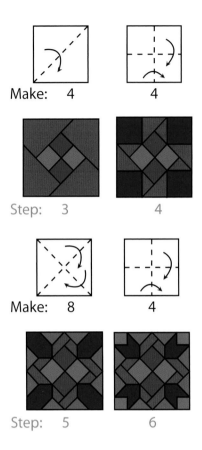

Make: 4   4

Step: 3   4

Make: 8   4

Step: 5   6

Baste the pieces onto your blocks.

ASSEMBLY

Adding a sleeve to the BREEZE CATCHER

Make a sleeve and hanger for the top block (page 83).

Preparing the top and bottom blocks of the TRINKET BOX

The plain quilted square, which will form the bottom of the box, and the finished block, which will be the lid, must be finished slightly larger than the rest. This is so the 4 walls will sit on the base and the lid will not fall into the box.

Sew 1⅝" x 5½" (sides) and 1⅝" x 6½" (top and bottom) binding strips around the 2 squares. Lay the thin strips of batting around each of the 2 squares on top of the wrong side of the binding, wrap the binding over the batting, and topstitch or slipstitch the binding in place, depending on your finishing preference.

Preparing the remaining blocks

Bind the remaining blocks with the 1¼" x 4½" (sides) and 1¼" x 5½" (top and bottom) binding strips.

Connecting the blocks

BREEZE CATCHER

Select a very strong thread or monofilament (test for breakage) to join the blocks in sequence. Hide the knot in the binding of the lower corner of the first block, opposite the sleeve, and secure the thread well. String a bead onto the thread, then sew through the top corner of the next block. Secure well and hide the thread end between the layers. In the same manner, attach the remaining 4 blocks. Knot well and frequently to minimize sagging.

TRINKET BOX

Take the Step 2, 3, 4, and 5 blocks and sew them together with a doubled thread, edge to edge, with a ladder stitch. Join block 2 to block 5 to complete the sides of the box. Place the square onto the base (the Step 1 quilted block) and sew all 4 edges to the base. Finally, sew one edge of the finished block onto the edge of the block you want at the back of the box.

SHOPPING BAG

SHOPPING BAG, 16 ½" x 17" x 6",
MADE BY THE AUTHORS

Stores everywhere are selling reusable bags these days, gradually replacing the flimsy plastic ones that have been the North American norm for so long. Although the new sturdy bags are great for groceries, when you go shopping with the girls or need a bag to carry a few things to a friend's house, you might want something with a bit more flair that doesn't advertise where you shop.

This bag is beautiful as well as sturdy because, while the blocks are made of quilting cotton, the bag is a double layer of heavyweight denim.

MATERIALS

Fabric requirements (based on fabric at least 40" wide)

Amount	Color	Block Color Code
95"	dark, heavy denim	
22"	light orange/cream	A
13"	blue*	B
10"	dark green	C (Winged)
9"	light green	D (Mosaic)
11"	orange/rust	D (Winged)
15"	very dark green (for inner border)	

*The blocks were made with at least 3 different shades of hand-dyed scraps. Yardage and directions are given for one blue only.

Additional supplies

One decorative antique or new brass button (at least ¾")
2 flat dark brown buttons (approximately ¾")
12" heavyweight black elastic thread (approximately ³⁄₁₆")
Contrasting thread for quilting
40 wooden beads (approximately ⅛") to embellish the blocks and cornerstones
Optional: 4 brass spacers (placed under the 4 beads on the cornerstones)
2 pieces 5" x 15" plastic cardboard (³⁄₁₆" thick) cut so the grain is going in opposite directions

CUTTING DIRECTIONS

Tote components

From the denim, cut and label:

2	1¼" x 15"	(nine-block unit border)
2	1¼" x 16½"	(nine-block unit border)
1	16½" x 16½"	(nine-block unit back)
2	16½" x 39½"	(bag front-bottom-back)
4	6½" x 16½"	(bag sides)
2	3" x 19"	(bag handles)
1	6½" x 34"	(bottom insert)

Sashing, cornerstones, and borders

For the orange sashing, cut:

12	1⅛" x 4½"

For the blue cornerstones, cut

4	1⅛" x 1⅛"

From the very dark green, cut:

2 strips	1¼" x 13½"	(border)
2 strips	1¼" x 15"	(border)
3 strips	1¾" x 40"	(binding)

Folded blocks

Mosaic-easy

Step	Color	# of Pcs	Size	Folding Code
1	A	1	4½" x 4½"	-
2	A, D	2 ea	2¾" x 4½"	I
3	B	4	2¾" x 4½"	D
4	A, D	2 ea	2¾" x 2¾"	C
5*	D	4	1¾" x 1¾"	B

* Optional–not on tote.

Winged Four-Patch-easy

Step	Color	# of Pcs	Size	Folding Code
1	A	1	4½" x 4½"	-
2	A, C	2 ea	4½" x 4½"	A
3	D	4	2½" x 4½"	D
4	B	4	2½" x 2½"	C
5*	A, C	2 ea	2½" x 2½"	A

* For center block, cut 4 of color A.

Cut the components for 5 Winged Four-Patch blocks and 4 Mosaic blocks.

Shopping Bag

Folded blocks

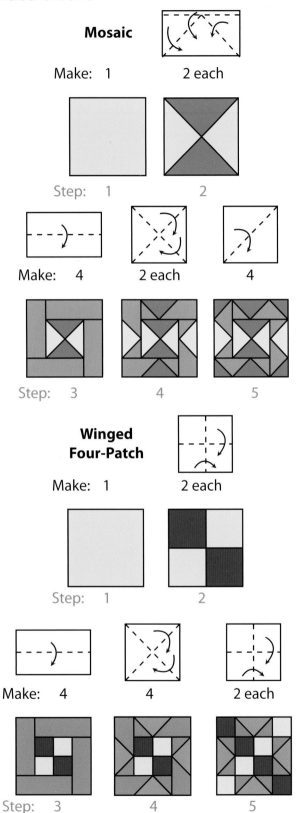

Note: We eliminated the last step of the Mosaic block to emphasize the diagonal lines.

Make 5 Winged Four-Patch blocks and 4 Mosaic blocks, referring to the color codes and folding diagrams.

Add beads at the triangle points so the thread passes through the tip of each triangle.

Lay out the blocks, the 1⅛" x 4½" sashing strips, and the 1⅛" x 1⅛" cornerstones as shown. Join them in rows, then join the rows.

Add beads to the cornerstones.

Add the 13½" x 1¼" border strips to the sides and the 15" x 1¼" border strips to the top and bottom of the nine-block unit.

Preparing the shopping bag components

Front pocket

Add the 15" x 1¼" denim border strips to the sides and the 16½" x 1¼" strips to the top and the bottom of the nine-block unit. (Refer to the instructions for adding borders to folded-block sashing, page 82). Press the seams toward the denim.

Place the nine-block unit right sides together with the 16½" x 16½" denim backing, and stitch along the top and bottom edges. Press these seams open, then turn right-side out. Lay the pocket flat with the nine-block unit facing up and press the seamed edges flat to complete the front pocket.

Bag front, back, and bottom

Place the two 16½" x 39½" denim rectangles right sides together, and stitch along the short edges. Press the seams open and turn right-side out. Line up the 2 seams so that they are at the center of the piece and press flat. (This seam will run along the bottom of the bag.)

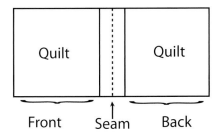

Pin baste and quilt the front and the back of the bag, leaving the bottom of the bag unquilted (approximately 3" on either side of the seam).

Note: If you choose not to quilt the layers, topstitch the pressed fold at both ends to keep them from shifting.

Bag sides

Pin 2 pairs of 16½" x 6½" denim rectangles right sides together and stitch each along one short end. Press the seams open. Fold along the seams and press again. Quilt as desired.

Note: In case of directional quilting, the fold is at the top edge of the bag.

Bag handles

Press under ¼" along both long edges of the two 3" x 19" denim rectangles. Fold in half along the length, press, and topstitch down the open edge of each. Fold over 1" at the short ends of both handles and press.

Bag assembly

Attaching the handles

Lay the bag right-side down on your work surface. Measure 3½" from the center point of the finished edges and mark with a pin or chalk. Position the center of the ends of each handle on the marks with the folded end against the bag. Pin in place and stitch each end securely to the bag with a square and an X, as shown on page 36. Use coordinating thread in the bobbin and on top, since the stitching is exposed on both sides.

Shopping Bag

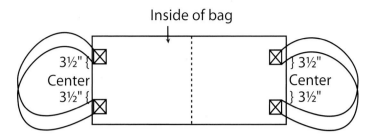

Attaching the pocket

Position the pocket on the outside front of the bag so that the top edge of the pocket is ½" from the finished edge of the bag and the raw edges line up along the sides. Pin in place on all sides. Topstitch along the bottom edge only with coordinating thread. Stitching twice is recommended.

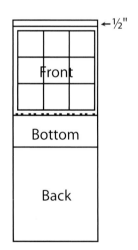

Inserting the sides

Place the bag right-side down on your work surface. Position a quilted side piece along the raw edge of the bag front, aligning the raw and finished edges. Pin, then baste in place, stopping 1" from the bottom corner as shown.

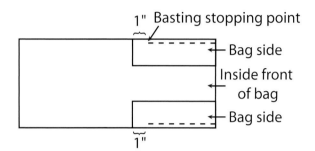

In the same way, position, pin, and baste the second side piece along the opposite raw edge of the bag front.

Fold the bag into a U shape, insides together, and pin the sides to the back edges of the bag in the same manner.

Pin and then baste around the corners and across the base of the bag on both sides, easing any excess across the bottom edges.

Make a long binding strip with the 1¾" x 40" strips and cut the strip in half. Position each strip along the raw edges so that its center lines up with the bottom of the back and there is a tail at each upper corner. Topstitch from the top of the bag, across the bottom, and up to the top again on both sides, folding under the ends of the binding at the top of the bag before stitching in place.

Note: The binding topstitch should be done from both outer facing sides of the bag.

Bottom insert

Zigzag stitch around all 4 edges of the remaining 6½" x 34" piece of denim. Fold in half across the width, right sides together, and sew both long sides with a ½" seam. Clip the corners, taking care not to cut the seam stitches, and turn it right-side out. Insert the two pieces of plastic cardboard.

Tuck in the unfinished edges. Position the insert in the base of your new bag.

FINISHING

Sew a decorative button onto the front pocket, centered on the top edge. Sew a flat button onto the inside of the front of the bag about 3" from the top edge, and another flat button on the inside of the back of the bag (optional).

Fold a 12" piece of elastic thread in half and place the loop over the decorative button. Run the elastic into the bag to the front inside button and mark the point where the button is attached. Stitch the folded thread together at the marked point and at a second spot so you have a loop big enough for the inside button(s) to pass through.

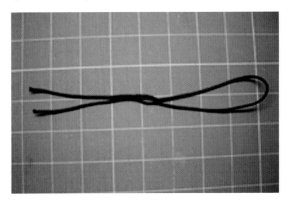

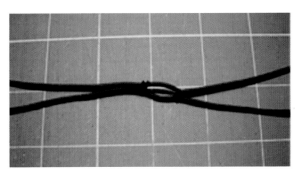

With the elastic looped over an inside button, bring the elastic out and over the decorative button. The loop can be fastened to either inside button.

FLANDERS FIELDS

FLANDERS FIELDS, 28½" x 24",
MADE BY THE AUTHORS

Each Remembrance Day, school children all over Canada recite Lieutenant Colonel John McCrae's poem "In Flanders Fields." Very few of us haven't been touched by war in some way, ourselves included, so this quilt was designed in honor and in memory of those who defend our freedom and the freedom of others.

This quilt includes the Canadian Gardens block as cornerstones to honor the Canadian-born doctor who wrote the poem; Poppy, Leaf, and Soldier's Cross for Flanders fields; and a yellow border for those waiting for someone to come home.

MATERIALS

Fabric requirements (based on fabric at least 40" wide)

Amount	Color
16"	red
12"	white
Assorted scraps of greens	
5"	brown
27"	blue
5"	yellow (inner border)
23"	dark blue (outer border and binding)
28"	backing

Additional supplies

Batting: 28" x 32"

CUTTING DIRECTIONS

Sashing, borders*, binding*, and sleeve

For the sashing, cut:
Blue

1	1⅛" x 24"	
2	1⅛" x 6½"	
2	1⅛" x 4¼"	
8	1⅛" x 4½"	

Light green

3	1⅛" x 1¼"

Medium green

1	1⅛" x 24"

For the yellow inner border, cut:

2	1" x 25"
2	1" x 21½"

From the dark blue, cut:

Border	4	3" x 26½"
Binding	2	1¼" x 28"
	2	1¼" x 32"
Sleeve	2	3" x 15"

*Measure across the width and length of your quilt top before trimming the borders and binding to their final lengths.

Folded blocks

Cut the components for the number of blocks indicated below, following the color codes in the charts on pages 40–41. Remember to multiply the number of pieces to cut by the number of blocks.

3 Poppy
4 Canadian Gardens
3 Leaf Block
4 Soldier's Cross

The colors for the Poppy block are: A/blue, B/red, C/green, D/brown. See page 27 for the Poppy cutting chart and folding diagram.

Flanders Fields

Canadian Gardens-intermediate

Step	Color	# of Pcs	Size	Folding Code
1	Red	1	4½" x 4½"	-
2	White	4	3½" x 3½"	B
3	Red	4	2½" x 4½"	D
4	White	4	2½" x 2½"	B
5	Red	4	2½" x 2½"	A
6	White	4	1½" x 1½"	B

Leaf Block-intermediate

Step	Color	# of Pcs	Size	Folding Code
1	Green	1	4½" x 4½"	-
2	Blue	2	3⅞" x 4½"	D
3	Green	2	4½" x 4½"	B
4	Green	2	3½" x 3½"	B
5	Green	2	2½" x 2½"	B
6	Blue	2	1½" x 1½"	B

CONSTRUCTION

Folded blocks

Follow the diagrams to make the 14 blocks.

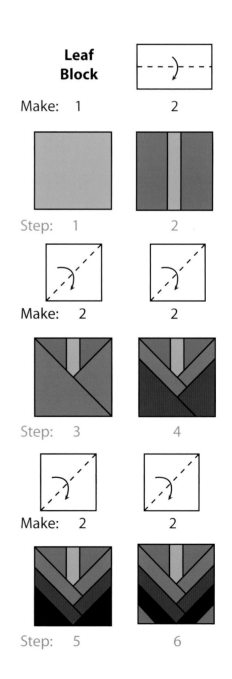

Canadian Gardens

Make: 1   4

Step: 1   2

Make: 4   4

Step: 3   4

Make: 4   4

Step: 5   6

Leaf Block

Make: 1   2

Step: 1   2

Make: 2   2

Step: 3   4

Make: 2   2

Step: 5   6

Soldiers's Cross-easy

Step	Color	# of Pcs	Size	Folding Code
1	White	1	4½" x 4½"	-
2	Blue	2	3⅞" x 5⅛"	E
3	Blue	2	2¾" x 3⅞"	E
4	Blue	2	1⅝" x 4½"	D

Grass and sky

Photocopy or trace the pattern for the grass and sky sections (page 42) onto the weight of paper you prefer for paper piecing. From your green scraps, paper piece the grass section. Paper piece the sky with your blue scraps. Trim both pieces to measure 4½" x 14½".

ASSEMBLY

Join the blocks, sashing, grass, and sky components into rows, and then join the rows. Add the inner and outer borders.

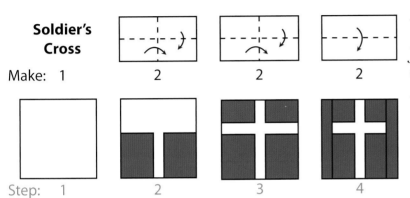

Soldier's Cross

Make: 1   2   2   2

Step: 1   2   3   4

Flanders Fields

Layer, quilt, add the split-sleeve, and bind.

In Flanders Fields

In Flanders Fields the poppies blow
Between the crosses, row on row,
That mark our place; and in the sky
The larks, still bravely singing, fly
Scarce heard amid the guns below.
We are the dead. Short days ago
We lived, felt dawn, saw sunset glow,
Loved, and were loved, and now we lie
In Flanders Fields.
Take up our quarrel with the foe:
To you from failing hands we throw
The torch; be yours to hold it high.
If ye break faith with us who die
We shall not sleep, though poppies grow
In Flanders Fields.

From *In Flanders Fields and Other Poems* by John McCrae,
G. P. Putnam's Sons, New York and London, The
Knickerbocker Press, 1919.

Grass

Enlarge 350%
Actual size should be
4½" x 14½ "

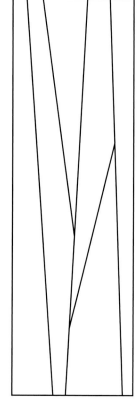

Sky

OMA'S BELL PULL

We can't begin to guess how many bell pulls our grandmothers and their daughters have cross-stitched and embroidered, or how often we've stopped in a hallway or nook to admire their lovely imagery through the years. Until now, neither of us has ever made a bell pull for ourselves, having no servants to ring for. (Unfortunately we have to scrub our own floors.) But even though our bell pull won't summon the butler, it will brighten up that little nook in need of some color.

OMA'S BELL PULL,
28½" x 24",
MADE BY THE AUTHORS

SANDHILLS

NORTHUMBERLAND STAR

SAINT GREGORY'S CROSS

FOUR-STAR FOX & GOOSE

MRS. KELLER'S NINE-PATCH

UNION SQUARES

STAR & SQUARE

SPARKLING SKIES

FOOL'S SQUARE

Oma's Bell Pull

This project's blocks are some of the more difficult ones in this book, so make sure you refer to the tips given with the first project on page 15 before attempting them. Once the blocks are complete, the construction is simple.

MATERIALS

Fabric requirements (based on fabric at least 40" wide)

Amount	Color
20"	dark red
16"	orange
17"	deep yellow
20"	dark green
29"	cream

Additional supplies

6" bell pull hardware
Batting: 4½" x 41"

CUTTING DIRECTIONS

Sashing, backing, sleeves, and binding

For the dark red sashing and binding, cut:
8 strips	1⅛" x 4½"
2 strips	1¼" x 5½"
2 strips	1¼" x 43" (pieced)

For the cream backing*, cut:
| 1 strip | 6½" x 45" |

* Measure the length and width of your joined blocks before cutting.

For the cream sleeves, cut:
| 2 strips | 2" x 5" |

Folded blocks

Cut the components for 1 block each, following the color codes in the charts on pages 45–48.

The colors for the Sandhills block steps are: 1/orange, 2/orange & yellow, 3/red, 4/green, 5 & 6/cream. See pages 29–30 for the cutting chart and folding diagram.

The colors for the Union Squares block steps are: 1/orange, 2/cream, 3/green, 4 orange, 5, 6 & 7/yellow. See page 11 for the Union Squares cutting chart and folding diagram.

CONSTRUCTION

Folded blocks

Follow the folding diagrams to make the blocks.

Use the line drawings in the folding diagrams for placement of the block components, not the quilt photo, since there are a few mistakes in our bell pull that you're not supposed to notice!

Before sewing step 2 of Saint Gregory's Cross, refer to page 15 for an important tip for blocks where step 2 doesn't cover the perimeter of the basic square.

Northumberland Star-intermediate

Step	Color	# of Pcs	Size	Folding Code
1	Cream	1	4½" x 4½"	-
2	Green	4	3½" x 3½"	B
3	Cream	4	3½" x 3½"	A
4	Green	4	2½" x 2½"	B
5	Yellow	4	2½" x 2½"	C
6	Yellow	4	2½" x 2½"	A

Saint Gregory's Cross-intermediate

Step	Color	# of Pcs	Size	Folding Code
1	Cream	1	4½" x 4½"	-
2	Green	4	3¼" x 3¼"	A
3	Yellow	4	2½" x 2½"	B
4	Orange	4	3¼" x 3¼"	C
5	Cream	4	1⅞" x 1⅞"	C
6	Green	4	1¼" x 1¼"	B

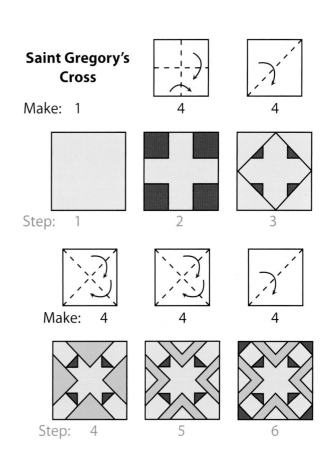

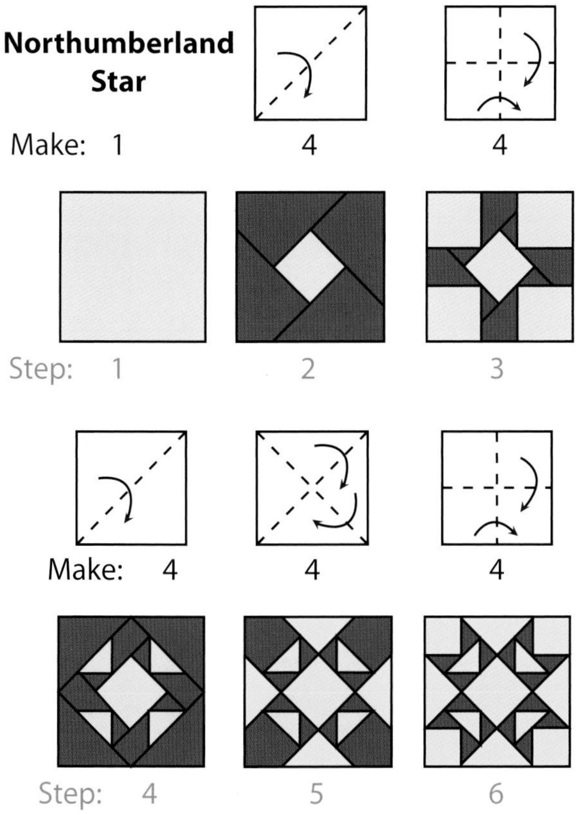

Oma's Bell Pull

Four-Star Fox & Goose-intermediate

Step	Color	# of Pcs	Size	Folding Code
1	Cream	1	4½" x 4½"	-
2	Green	4	3½" x 3½"	B
3	Yellow	4	2½" x 4½"	D
4	Orange	4	2½" x 2½"	C
5	Green	4	2½" x 2½"	A
6	Orange	4	1½" x 1½"	B

Mrs. Keller's Nine-Patch-advanced

Step	Color	# of Pcs	Size	Folding Code
1	Cream	1	4½" x 4½"	-
2	Green	4	3¾" x 4½"	D
3	Yellow	4	2⅛" x 4½"	D
4	Orange	4	3¾" x 3¾"	A
5	Cream	4	2¼" x 2¼"	B
6	Red	4	2¼" x 2¼"	A
7	Cream	4	1⅜" x 1⅜"	B

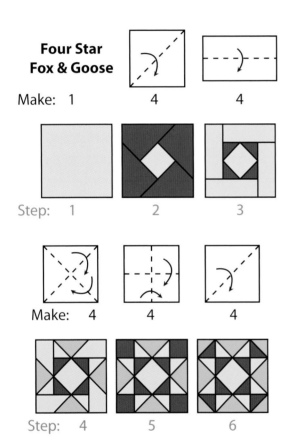

Four Star Fox & Goose

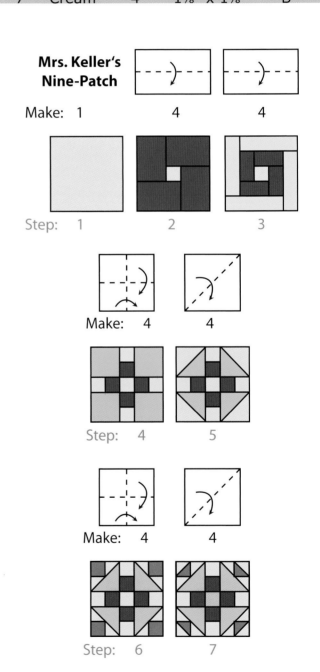

Mrs. Keller's Nine-Patch

Star & Square-advanced

Step	Color	# of Pcs	Size	Folding Code
1	Red	1	4½" x 4½"	-
2*	Orange	4	2⅛" x 3⅜"	I
3	Cream	4	3¼" x 3¼"	A
4	Green	4	2½" x 2½"	C
5	Green	4	1¾" x 1¾"	B
6	Cream	4	1¾" x 1¾"	A
7	Red	4	1⅛" x 1⅛"	B

Sparkling Skies-advanced

Step	Color	# of Pcs	Size	Folding Code
1	Cream	1	4½" x 4½"	-
2	Orange	4	3⅝" x 3⅝"	B
3	Green	4	3⅛" x 3⅛"	B
4	Cream	4	2" x 2"	C
5	Cream	4	3⅛" x 3⅛"	A
6	Yellow	4	1¾" x 3"	E
7	Yellow	4	1¾" x 3"	E

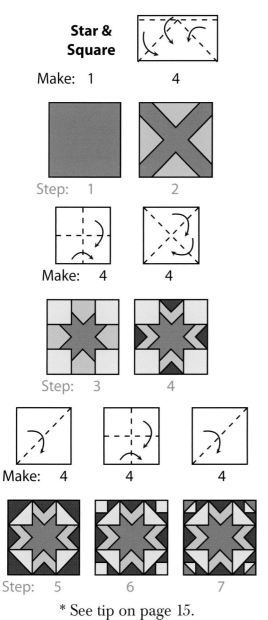

Star & Square

Make: 1   4

Step: 1   2

Make: 4   4

Step: 3   4

Make: 4   4   4

Step: 5   6   7

* See tip on page 15.

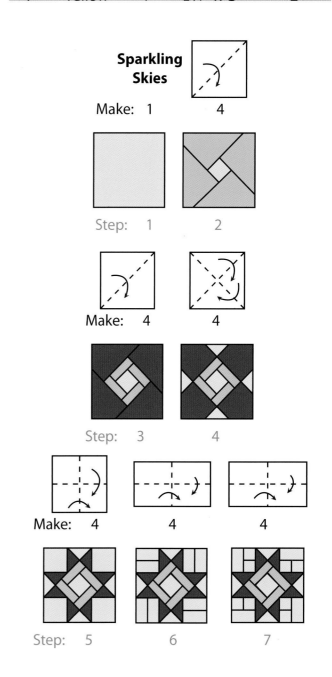

Sparkling Skies

Make: 1   4

Step: 1   2

Make: 4   4

Step: 3   4

Make: 4   4   4

Step: 5   6   7

Oma's Bell Pull

Fool's Square-advanced

Step	Color	# of Pcs	Size	Folding Code
1	Cream	1	4½" x 4½"	-
2	Orange	4	3¾" x 4½"	D
3	Red	4	3¾" x 3¾"	A
4	Green	4	2⅛" x 4½"	D
5	Yellow	4	2⅞" x 2⅛"	H
6	Orange	4	2⅛" x 2⅛"	A
7	Cream	4	1⅜" x 1⅜"	B

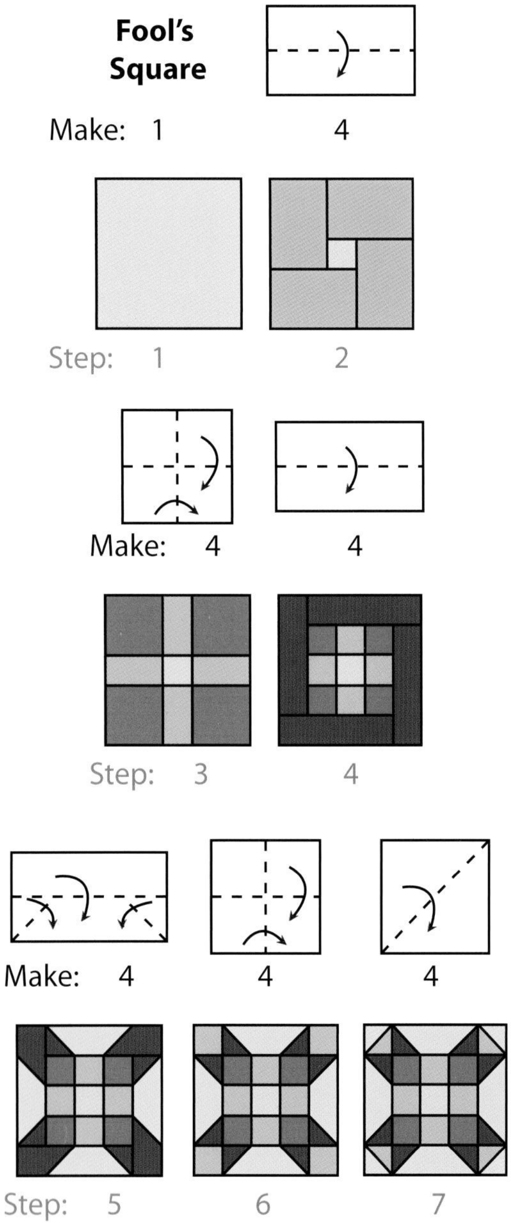

FINISHING

Join the blocks together with the sashing, add the batting, backing, and the top and bottom sleeves (no need for the split sleeve with bell pull hardware), and bind.

Fool's Square

Make: 1   4

Step: 1   2

Make: 4   4

Step: 3   4

Make: 4   4   4

Step: 5   6   7

Salute to the Neighbors

This pennant-shaped wallhanging was designed using the colors of the United States, our neighbor to the south, but they are also the colors of the flag of our birthplace, The Netherlands. The blocks were chosen because of their American names. They are all six- and seven-step blocks and are among the more difficult ones in this book. However, construction of the pennant is simple.

Salute to the Neighbors, 14" x 24",
MADE BY THE AUTHORS

Salute to the Neighbors

MATERIALS

Fabric requirements (based on fabric at least 40" wide)

Amount	Color	Cut
1¼ yards	white*	50" x 40"
½ yard	red	18" x 40"
½ yard	blue	16" x 40"

* includes 16" x 27" backing and binding

Additional supplies

Batting: 16" x 27"
Silver metallic thread (for quilting)

CUTTING DIRECTIONS

Sashing, cornerstones, and setting triangles

From the red, cut:
26 sashing strips   4½" by 1⅛"

From the blue, cut:
18 cornerstones   1⅛" x 1⅛"

From the white (see the layout diagram, page 53), cut:

2	4½" x 4½" (position A)
1	8" x 8", cut twice on the diagonal (position B)
1	5½" x 5½", cut in half on the diagonal (position C; you will use only one)
1	5" x 5", cut in half on the diagonal (position (D)

Note: The setting triangles are cut generously; trim the quilt top after the pieces are joined.

Binding and split sleeve

For the binding, cut:
2 strips   1¼" x 40"

For the split sleeve, cut:
2 strips   7½" x 4"

Folded blocks

To create the red-white-and-blue color scheme, some of the blocks are made with fewer colors than they traditionally would be. Refer to the cutting charts to cut components for 1 of each of these blocks. See pages 51 and 52 for the Northumberland Star cutting chart and folding diagram.

CONSTRUCTION

Folded blocks

Follow the folding diagrams to make the blocks.

Assembly

Lay out the components as shown on page page 53, and join into rows. Join the rows. Trim.

Finishing

Layer, quilt, add the split sleeve, and bind.

Missouri Star–intermediate

Step	Color	# of Pcs	Size	Folding Code
1	Blue	1	4½" x 4½"	-
2	Red	4	3½" x 3½"	B
3	Blue	4	2½" x 4½"	D
4	Red	4	2½" x 2½"	B
5	White	4	2½" x 2½"	C
6	White	4	2½" x 2½"	A

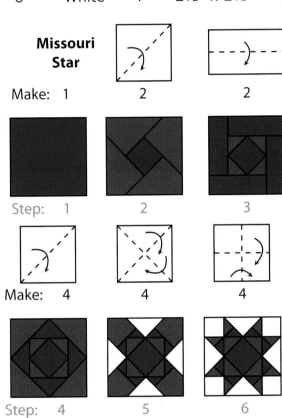

Missouri Star

Make: 1   2   2

Step: 1   2   3

Make: 4   4   4

Step: 4   5   6

Ohio Star Variation–intermediate

Step	Color	# of Pcs	Size	Folding Code
1	Red	1	4½" x 4½"	-
2	Blue	4	3¼" x 4½"	D
3	Red	4	3¼" x 3¼"	B
4	White	4	2" x 2"	C
5	White	4	3¼" x 3¼"	A
6	Blue	4	1⅞" x 1⅞"	B

Salute to the Neighbors

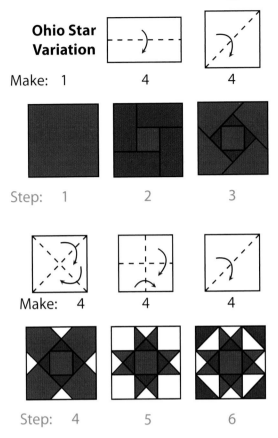

Ohio Star Variation

Make: 1   4   4

Step: 1   2   3

Make: 4   4   4

Step: 4   5   6

Northumberland Star–intermediate

Step	Color	# of Pcs	Size	Folding Code
1	Red	1	4½" x 4½"	-
2	Blue	4	3½" x 3½"	B
3	Red	4	3½" x 3½"	A
4	Blue	4	2½" x 2½"	B
5	White	4	2½" x 2½"	C
6	White	4	2½" x 2½"	A

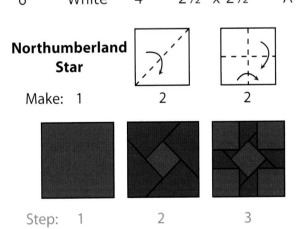

Northumberland Star

Make: 1   2   2

Step: 1   2   3

Salute to the Neighbors

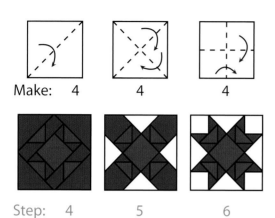

Make: 4   4   4

Step: 4   5   6

Oregon Trail-advanced

Step	Color	# of Pcs	Size	Folding Code
1	Red	1	4½" x 4½"	-
2	White	4	3¼" x 4½"	D
3	Blue	4	3¼" x 3¼"	A
4	Red	4	1⅞" x 4½"	D
5	White	4	1⅞" x 2½"	G-1
6	White	4	1⅞" x 2½"	G-2
7	Blue	4	1⅞" x 1⅞"	A

Salt Lake City–intermediate

Step	Color	# of Pcs	Size	Folding Code
1	Red	1	4½" x 4½"	-
2	White	4	3½" x 3½"	B
3	Blue	4	2½" x 4½"	D
4	Red	4	2½" x 2½"	C
5	White	8	1½" x 1½"	C
6	White	4	1½" x 1½"	B

Oregon Trail

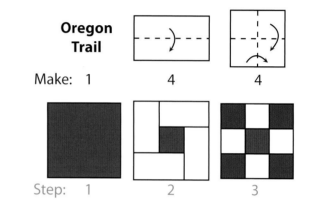

Make: 1   4   4

Step: 1   2   3

Salt Lake City

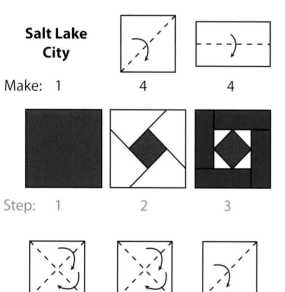

Make: 1   4   4

Step: 1   2   3

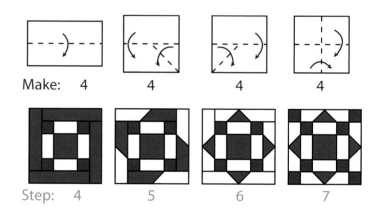

Make: 4   4   4   4

Step: 4   5   6   7

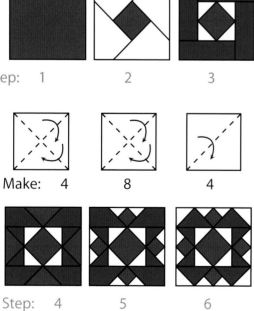

Make: 4   8   4

Step: 4   5   6

Salute to the Neighbors

State of Illinois-advanced

Step	Color	# of Pcs	Size	Folding Code
1	Blue	1	4½" x 4½"	-
2	White	4	3⅞" x 3⅞"	B
3	Red	4	3¼" x 4½"	D
4	White	4	3¼" x 3¼"	B
5	Red	4	1⅞" x 4½"	D
6	White	4	2½" x 2½"	B
7	Blue	4	3¼" x 3¼"	A
8	White	4	1⅞" x 1⅞"	B

State of Illinois

Make: 1   4   4   4

Step: 1   2   3   4

Make: 4   4   4   4

Step: 5   6   7   8

Philadelphia Pavements–intermediate

Step	Color	# of Pcs	Size	Folding Code
1	Red	1	4½" x 4½"	-
2	White	4	3½" x 4½"	D
3	Blue	4	3½" x 3½"	A
4	Red	4	2¾" x 2¾"	B
5	White	4	1½" x 4½"	D
6	Blue	4	1½" x 1½"	A

Philadelphia Pavements

Make: 1   4   4

Step: 1   2   3

Make: 4   4   4

Step: 4   5   6

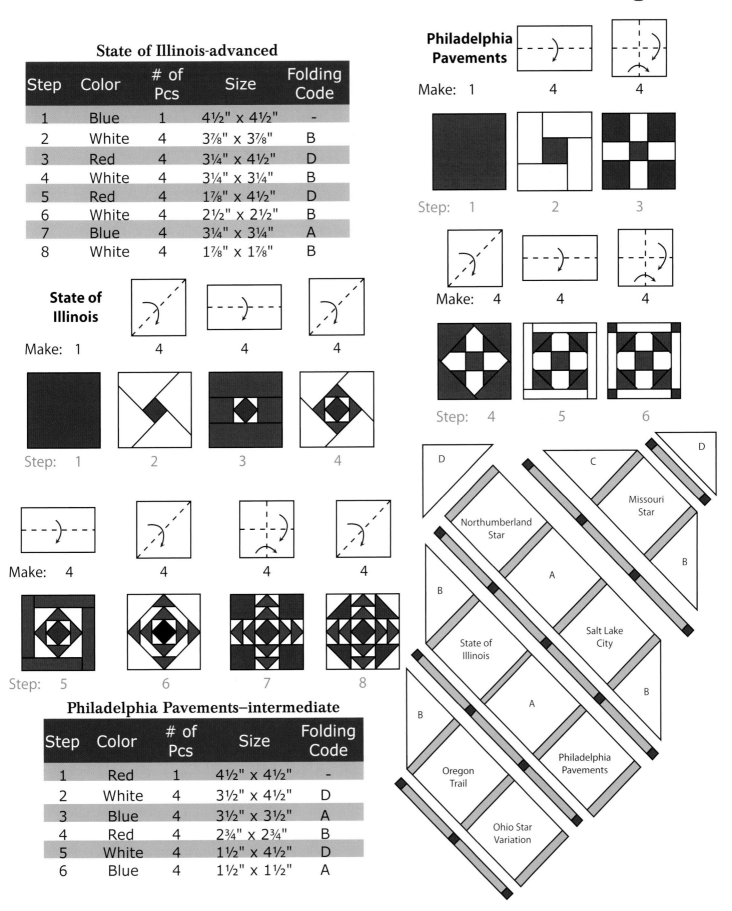

D

Northumberland Star

C

Missouri Star

B

B

A

State of Illinois

Salt Lake City

B

B

A

Oregon Trail

Philadelphia Pavements

Ohio Star Variation

Color gradations, whether found in hand-dyed fabrics or commercial prints, can be used to add dimension to your work. This runner features five seven-step color gradations. The light-to-dark transition makes each Log Cabin Variation block virtually glow in its black setting. Although the block is simple, the number of layers involved and the way the blocks are set into the black background (with Y-seams) make this a challenging project for beginners.

GEMSTONES, 9" x 38¼",
MADE BY THE AUTHORS

MATERIALS

Fabric requirements

7 fat eighths of a seven-step gradation in five different colors–green, orange, red, violet, and blue
OR
use fabric at least 40" wide and cut the amounts given.

Amount	Color	Block Color Code
3" x 18"	very light	A
4" x 18"	light	B
4" x 18"	medium light	C
5" x 18"	medium	D
5" x 18"	medium dark	E
6" x 18"	dark	F
6" x 6"	very dark	G

1 yard black

Additional supplies

Batting: 13" x 42"
Freezer paper for templates (templates include ¼" seam allowance)
Quilting thread (We used rayon thread in a sand color.)

CUTTING DIRECTIONS

Templates, backing, sleeves, and binding

From the black, cut:
1 backing	11" x 40"
3 binding strips	1¼" x 40"
1 sleeve	5½" x 5½"
Template A	1 right-side up and 1 reverse
Template B	2 right-side up and 2 reverse
Template C	1 right-side up and 1 reverse
Template D	2 right-side up and 2 reverse

Folded blocks

Cut the components for a Log Cabin Variation block in each of the 5 colorways.

CONSTRUCTION

Log Cabin Variation-advanced

Step	Color	# of Pcs	Size	Folding Code
1	G	1	4½" x 4½"	-
2	F	4	4" x 4"	B
3	E	4	3½" x 3½"	B
4	D	4	3" x 3"	B
5	C	4	2½" x 2½"	B
6	B	4	2" x 2"	B
7	A	4	1½" x 1½"	B

Folded blocks

Follow the diagrams to make the 5 Log Cabin Variation blocks, each in a different color.

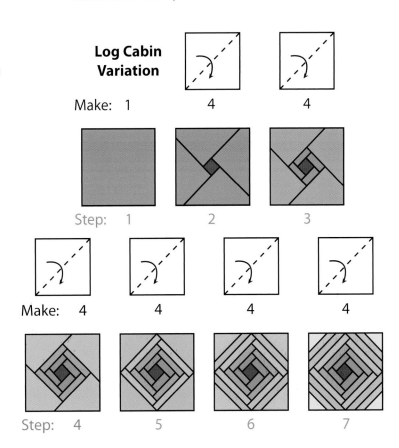

Log Cabin Variation

Make: 1   4   4
Step: 1   2   3

Make: 4   4   4   4
Step: 4   5   6   7

Gemstones

ASSEMBLY

Although you may be tempted to change the sewing order, we tried several ways and this order works best when dealing with thick folded blocks.

Lay out your blocks and background pieces as shown. Join the background pieces in pairs, starting and stopping ¼" from the ends; backstitch at both ends of the seams. Press the seams open.

Join the blocks to the background pieces in the sequence shown using Y-seams.

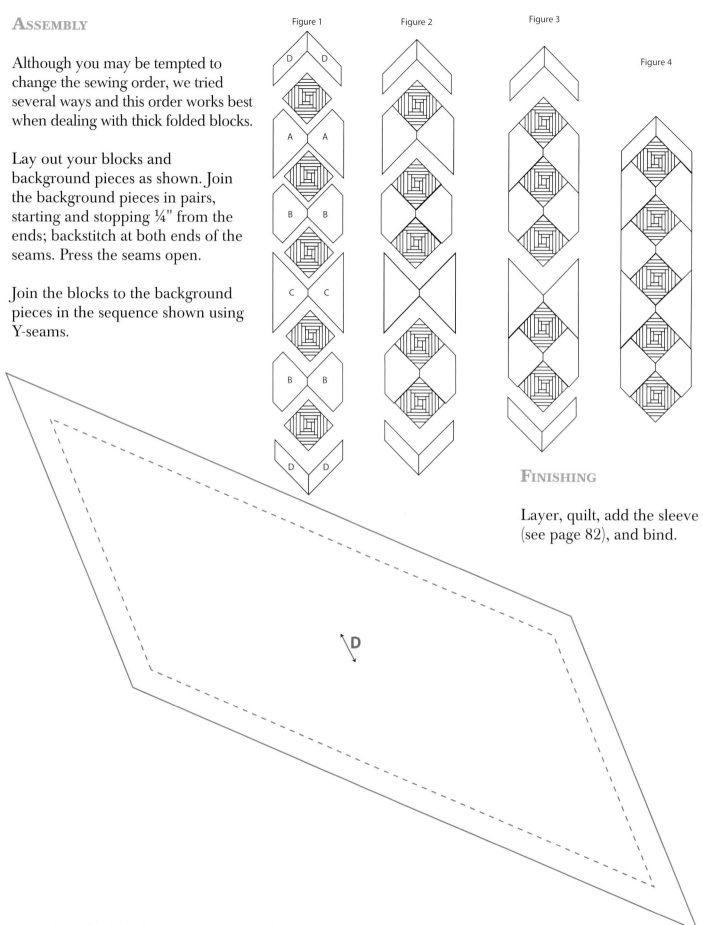

Figure 1 Figure 2 Figure 3 Figure 4

FINISHING

Layer, quilt, add the sleeve (see page 82), and bind.

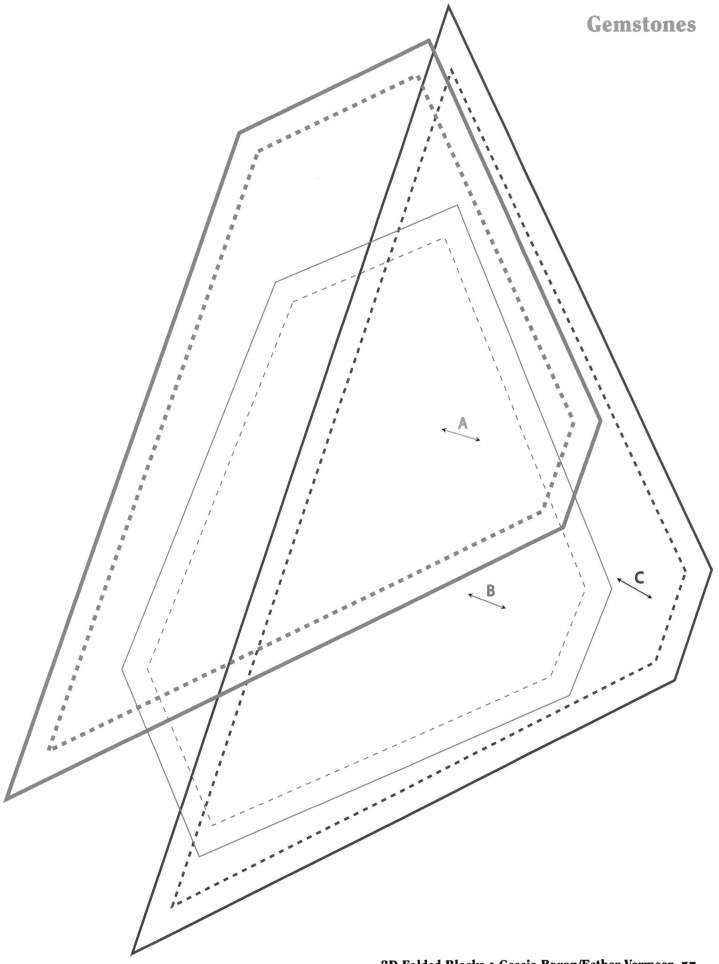

A

B

C

3D Folded Blocks • Geesje Baron/Esther Vermeer 57

STASHBUSTER, 26" x 30½",
MADE BY THE AUTHORS

The 30 blocks in this scrappy sampler range from simple to difficult; however, the construction of the quilt is simple and requires no quilting. The color scheme is based on color temperature (that is, red hot and cool blue) more than on value (light, medium, dark).

If you are looking for a project to shrink down the size of your scrap heap, this one fits the bill perfectly. The pieces are so small that once folded, even fabrics you're not particularly fond of will disappear into this color collage.

MATERIALS

Fabric requirements

Yardage is based on fabric at least 40" wide and indicates only how much fabric was actually used, not the size of the scrap collection from which the fabrics were selected. Working from scaps, you will need more than this, but how much depends on the size of your scraps and whether you want to use the same fabric in more than one block.

Yardage or assorted scraps of the following:

Amount	Color	Block Color Code
53"	cream	A
18"	yellow	B
38"	red	C
25"	green	D
39"	blue	E

Multicolor:
8" (binding)
28" (backing & split sleeve)

Additional supplies

Batting: 30" x 34"

CUTTING DIRECTIONS

Sashing, cornerstones, backing, sleeves, and binding

From the blue, cut:
49 sashing strips	1⅛" x 4½"
4 borders	2" x 31"

For the cornerstones, cut 5:
Cream	1⅛" x 1⅛"
Yellow	1⅛" x 1⅛"
Red	1⅛" x 1⅛"
Green	1⅛" x 1⅛"

For the multicolor backing and split sleeve, cut:
1	28" x 33"
2	13" x 6"

For the binding, cut
3 strips	1¼" x 40"

Folded blocks

Sort your scraps into 5 color groups and start pulling fabrics for each block, keeping in mind that Step 1 is always a 4½" x 4½" square and that Steps 2 and 3 will typically require more fabric than Steps 5 and 6. In the blocks marked with an * on the assembly diagram (page 72), the basic square is covered up and never seen again, so if you have a limited supply of a certain fabric, you can substitute another fabric for your basic square in those blocks without affecting the final look.

See the pages indicated on the chart for instructions for the 6 blocks introduced in other projects. See pages 60–71 for the instructions for the remaining 24 blocks.

Pg.	Block	Step 1	Step 2	Step 3	Step 4	Step 5	Step 6	Step 7
52	Oregon Trail	Green	Yellow	Red	Blue	Cream	Cream	Red
33 & 34	Mosaic	Cream	2 Cream & 2 Green	Cream	Blue	Red		
45	Saint Gregory's Cross	Cream	Blue	Yellow	Red	Cream	Green	
40	Canadian Gardens	Blue	Red	Green	Cream	Red	Cream	
46	Four-Star Fox & Goose	Red	Blue	Cream	Green	Blue	Yellow	
51	Ohio Star Variation	Cream	Red	Cream	Blue	Green	Yellow	

Stashbuster

Indian Meadows-advanced

Step	Color	# of Pcs	Size	Folding Code
1	Red	1	4½" x 4½"	-
2	Cream	2	3¾" x 3¾"	B
3	Blue	4	2⅛" x 4½"	D
4	Cream	2	3¾" x 3¾"	A
5	Yellow	4	2" x 2"	C
6	Yellow	2	2⅛" x 2⅛"	A
7	Green	2	2⅛" x 2⅛"	B

Ohio Star-easy

Step	Color	# of Pcs	Size	Folding Code
1	Red	1	4½" x 4½"	-
2	Cream	4	3¼" x 4½"	D
3	Blue	4	3¼" x 3¼"	B
4	Cream	4	1⅞" x 1⅞"	C
5	Green	4	3¼" x 3¼"	A

Indian Meadows

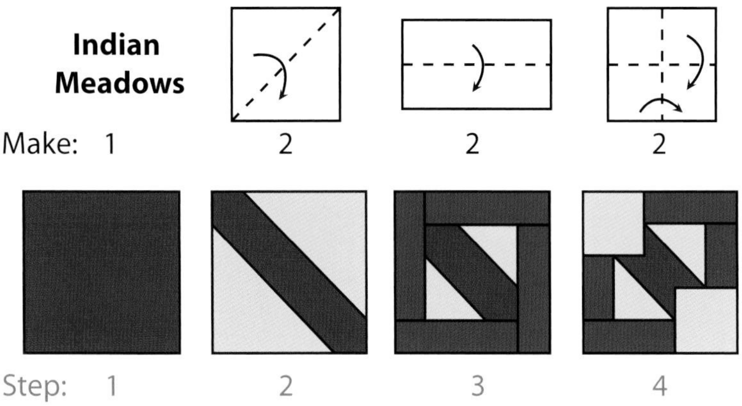

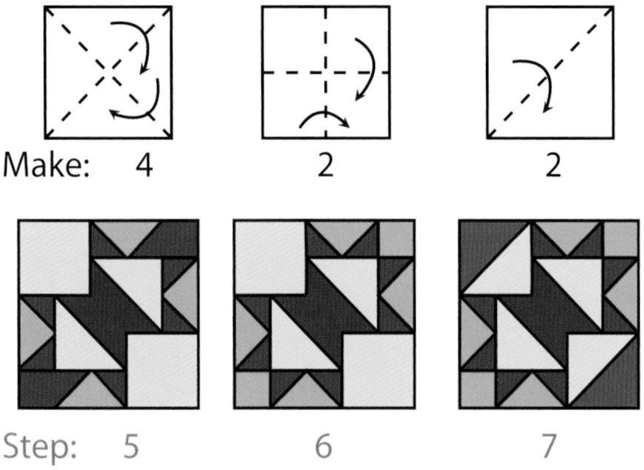

Make: 1 2 2 2

Ohio Star

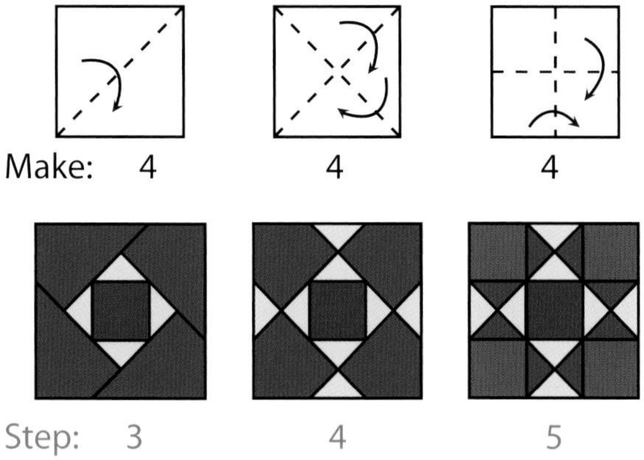

Make: 1 2

Step: 1 2 3 4

Step: 1 2

Make: 4 2 2

Make: 4 4 4

Step: 5 6 7

Step: 3 4 5

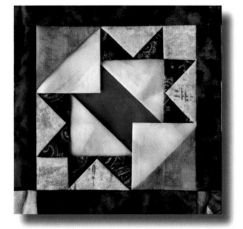

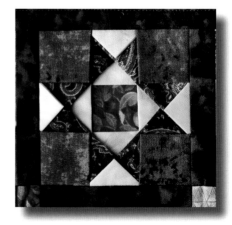

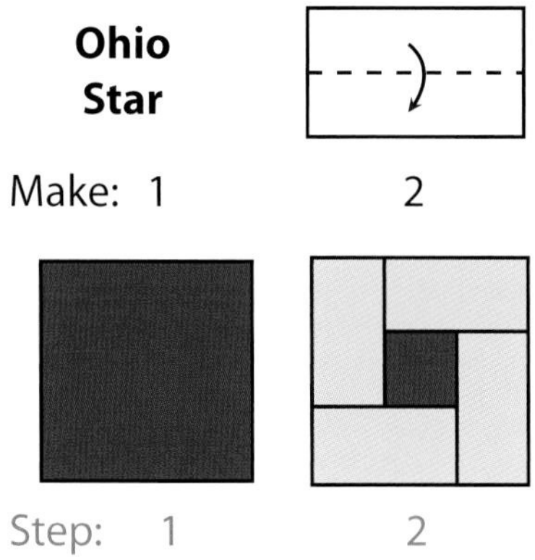

Double Wrench-easy

Step	Color	# of Pcs	Size	Folding Code
1	Red	1	4½" x 4½"	-
2	Cream	4	3⅝" x 4½"	D
3	Blue	4	2¼" x 4½"	D
4	Cream	4	3⅝" x 3⅝"	A
5	Green	4	2¼" x 2¼"	B

Winged Four-Patch-easy

Step	Color	# of Pcs	Size	Folding Code
1	Cream	1	4½" x 4½"	-
2	Cream, Red	2 ea	4½" x 4½"	A
3	Blue	4	2½" x 4½"	D
4	Yellow	4	2½" x 2½"	C
5	Red, Cream	2 ea	2½" x 2½"	A

Double Wrench

Make: 1 4 4

Step: 1 2 3

Make: 4 4

Step: 4 5

Winged Four-Patch

Make: 1 2 each 4

Step: 1 2 3

Make: 4 2 each

Step: 4 5

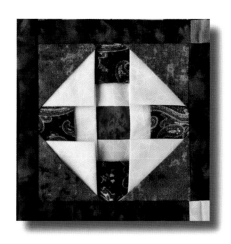

Stashbuster

Friendship Chain-easy

Step	Color	# of Pcs	Size	Folding Code
1	Cream	1	4½" x 4½"	-
2	Blue	4	3½" x 3½"	B
3	Yellow	2	2½" x 4½"	D
4	Red	4	2½" x 2½"	B
5	Cream	4	1½" x 1½"	B

Framed Nine-Patch-easy

Step	Color	# of Pcs	Size	Folding Code
1	Green	1	4½" x 4½"	-
2	Cream	4	3¼" x 4½"	D
3	Blue	4	3¼" x 3¼"	B
4	Cream	4	2¼" x 2¼"	B
5	Red	4	2¼" x 2¼"	A

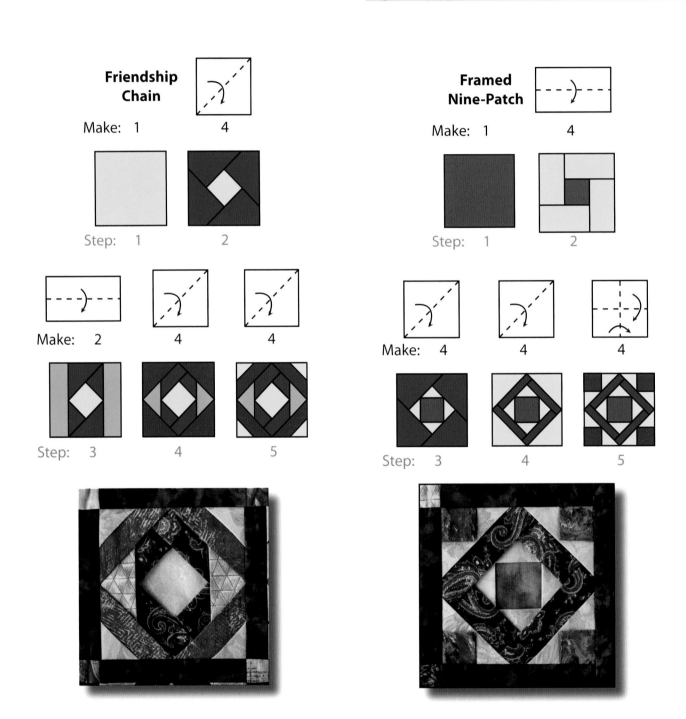

Block in a Block-easy

Step	Color	# of Pcs	Size	Folding Code
1	Cream	1	4½" x 4½"	-
2	Blue	4	3¼" x 4½"	D
3	Cream	4	3¼" x 3¼"	B
4	Red	4	2" x 4½"	D
5	Yellow	4	2" x 2"	B

Colonial Pavement-easy

Step	Color	# of Pcs	Size	Folding Code
1	Green	1	4½" x 4½"	-
2	Red	4	4" x 4"	B
3	Cream	4	3½" x 3½"	B
4	Blue	4	2¼" x 2¼"	B
5	Yellow	4	1½" x 1½"	B

To get the pinwheel effect, add the Step 3, 4, 5 pieces together along each side in a **clockwise** direction.

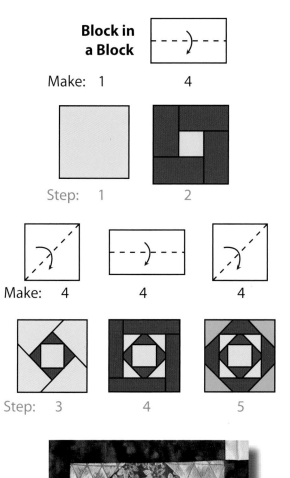

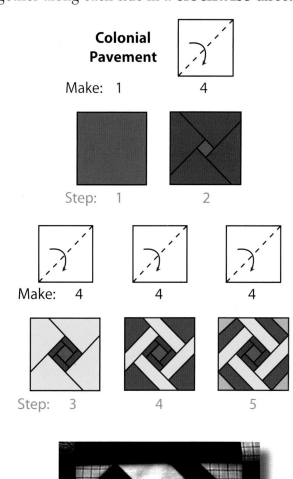

Stashbuster

Ribbon Quilt Block-easy

Step	Color	# of Pcs	Size	Folding Code
1	Cream	1	4½" x 4½"	-
2	Red	4	3¼" x 4½"	D
3	Blue	4	3¼" x 3¼"	G-2
4	Green	4	1⅞" x 1⅞"	B

Twin Darts-easy

Step	Color	# of Pcs	Size	Folding Code
1	Cream	1	4½" x 4½"	-
2	Cream, Red	2 ea	4½" x 4½"	A
3	Cream	2	3½" x 3½"	A
4	Blue	2	2¾" x 2¾"	B
5	Yellow, Red	2 ea	2¾" x 2¾"	A

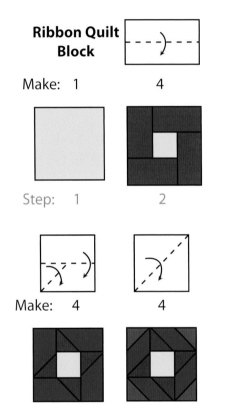

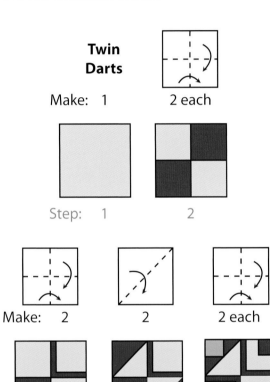

Card Basket-intermediate

Step	Color	# of Pcs	Size	Folding Code
1	Yellow	1	4½" x 4½"	-
2	Green	4	4" x 4"	B
3	Cream	4	3¼" x 3¼"	B
4	Blue	4	2" x 2"	C
5	Blue	4	3¼" x 3¼"	A
6	Red	4	1⅞" x 1⅞"	B

Mosaic Rose-intermediate

Step	Color	# of Pcs	Size	Folding Code
1	Cream	1	4½" x 4½"	-
2	Blue	4	3½" x 3½"	B
3	Yellow	4	2½" x 4½"	D
4	Red	4	2½" x 2½"	B
5	Cream	4	1½" x 1½"	B
6	Blue	4	1" x 1"	B

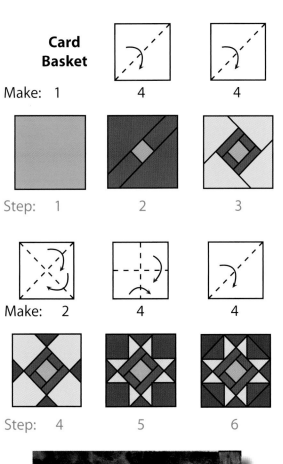

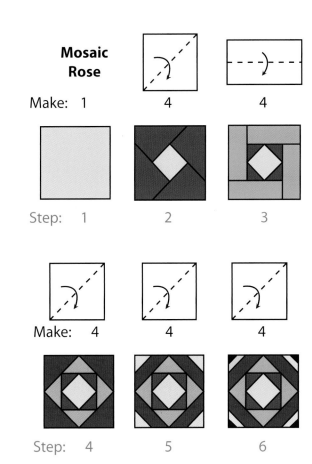

Stashbuster

Weathervane-easy

Step	Color	# of Pcs	Size	Folding Code
1	Blue	1	4½" x 4½"	-
2	Red	4	3¼" x 4½"	D
3	Green	4	3¼" x 3¼"	A
4	Cream	8	1⅞" x 1⅞"	C
5	Yellow	4	1⅞" x 1⅞"	A

Eight-Pointed Star-easy

Step	Color	# of Pcs	Size	Folding Code
1	Cream	1	4½" x 4½"	-
2	Blue	4	3½" x 3½"	B
3	Cream	4	2½" x 4½"	D
4	Red	4	1¾" x 2½"	I
5	Green	4	2½" x 2½"	A

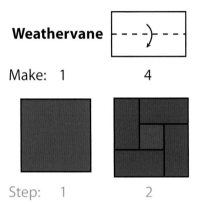

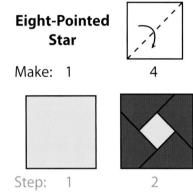

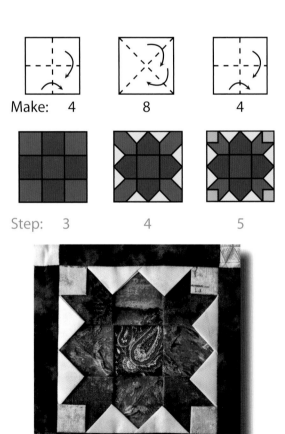

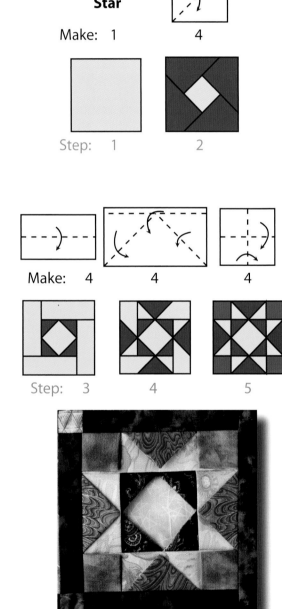

Old Maid's Puzzle-advanced

Step	Color	# of Pcs	Size	Folding Code
1	Cream	1	4½" x 4½"	-
2*	Red	2	3½" x 3½"	B
3	Cream	4	2½" x 4½"	D
4	Blue	2	4½" x 4½"	A
5	Yellow	2	2½" x 2½"	B
6	Red, Blue	2 ea	2½" x 2½"	A
7	Cream, Yellow	2 ea	1½" x 1½"	B

Puss in the Corner-intermediate

Step	Color	# of Pcs	Size	Folding Code
1	Blue	1	4½" x 4½"	-
2	Cream	4	3¼" x 4½"	D
3	Green	4	3¼" x 3¼"	B
4	Yellow	4	2½" x 2½"	B
5	Red	4	3¼" x 3¼"	A
6	Blue	4	2¼" x 2¼"	A

Old Maid's Puzzle

Make: 1   2   2   2

Step: 1   2   3   4

Make: 2   2 each   2 each

Step: 5   6   7

Puss in the Corner

Make: 1   4   4

Step: 1   2   3

Make: 4   4   4

Step: 4   5   6

* See page 15.

Stashbuster

Toad in the Puddle-easy

Step	Color	# of Pcs	Size	Folding Code
1	Cream	1	4½" x 4½"	-
2	Blue	4	3½" x 3½"	B
3	Cream	4	2½" x 4½"	D
4	Green	4	2½" x 2½"	B
5	Cream	4	1½" x 4½"	D

Grandmother's Choice-easy

Step	Color	# of Pcs	Size	Folding Code
1	Cream	1	4½" x 4½"	-
2	Blue	4	3⅝" x 4½"	D
3	Green	4	3⅝" x 3⅝"	A
4	Red	4	2¼" x 2¼"	B
5	Cream	4	2¼" x 2¼"	A

Toad in the Puddle

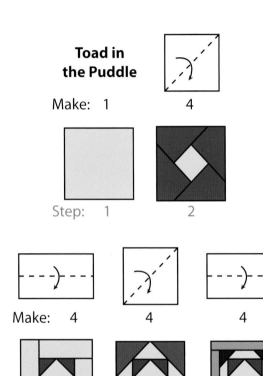

Grandmother's Choice

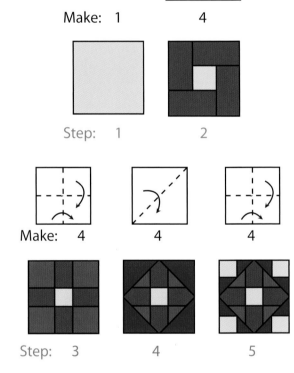

Tippecanoe & Tyler Too-intermediate

Step	Color	# of Pcs	Size	Folding Code
1	Green	1	4½" x 4½"	-
2	Cream	4	3½" x 3½"	B
3	Blue	4	2½" x 4½"	D
4	Cream	4	2½" x 2½"	A
5	Red	4	2½" x 2½"	C
6	Yellow	4	1½" x 1½"	B

Card Trick-easy

Step	Color	# of Pcs	Size	Folding Code
1	Cream	1	4½" x 4½"	-
2	Yellow, Green, Red, Blue	1 ea	4½" x 4½"	C
3	Yellow, Green, Red, Blue	1 ea	3¼" x 3¼"	B
4	Cream	4	2" x 2"	C
5	Cream	4	1⅞" x 1⅞"	B

Tippecanoe & Tyler Too

Make: 1   4   4

Step: 1   2   3

Make: 4   4   4

Step: 4   5   6

Card Trick

Make: 1   1 each

Step: 1   2

Make: 1 each   4   4

Step: 3   4   5

Stashbuster

Shoo Fly-easy

Step	Color	# of Pcs	Size	Folding Code
1	Cream	1	4½" x 4½"	-
2	Red	4	3¼" x 4½"	D
3	Cream	4	3¼" x 3¼"	A
4	Blue	4	1⅞" x 1⅞"	B

Old Favorite-advanced

Step	Color	# of Pcs	Size	Folding Code
1	Cream	1	4½" x 4½"	-
2	Blue	4	3½" x 4½"	D
3	Cream	4	3½" x 3½"	A
4	Red	4	2½" x 4½"	D
5	Yellow	4	2½" x 2½"	B
6	Green	4	1½" x 4½"	D
7	Cream	4	1½" x 1½"	A

Shoo Fly

Make: 1   4

Step: 1   2

Make: 4   4

Step: 3   4

Old Favorite

Make: 1   4   4

Step: 1   2   3

Make: 4   4   4   4

Step: 4   5   6   7

No Name-advanced

Step	Color	# of Pcs	Size	Folding Code
1	Blue	1	4½" x 4½"	-
2	Cream	4	3¼" x 4½"	D
3	Green	4	2¾" x 4½"	D
4	Blue	4	3⅛" x 3⅛"	C
5	Yellow	4	1½" x 4½"	D
6	Red	4	2⅛" x 2⅛"	B
7	Cream	4	2⅛" x 2⅛"	A

Hourglass-intermediate

Step	Color	# of Pcs	Size	Folding Code
1	Yellow	1	4½" x 4½"	-
2	Green	4	3½" x 3½"	B
3	Red	4	2½" x 4½"	D
4	Cream	4	2½" x 2½"	B
5	Blue	4	2½" x 2½"	A
6	Cream	4	1½" x 1½"	B

No Name

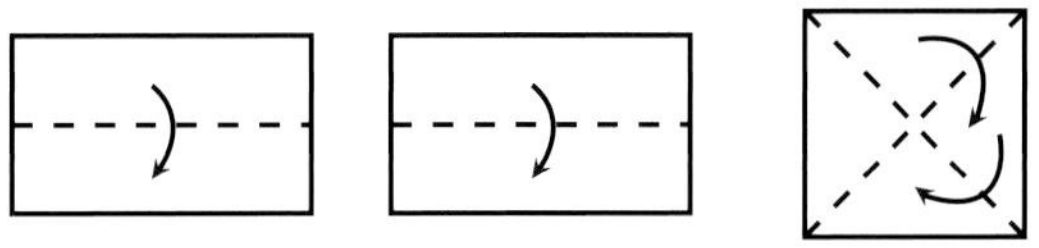

Make: 1   4   4   4

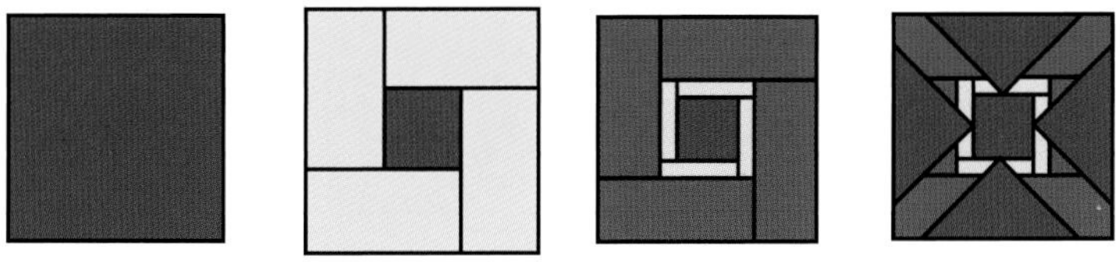

Hourglass

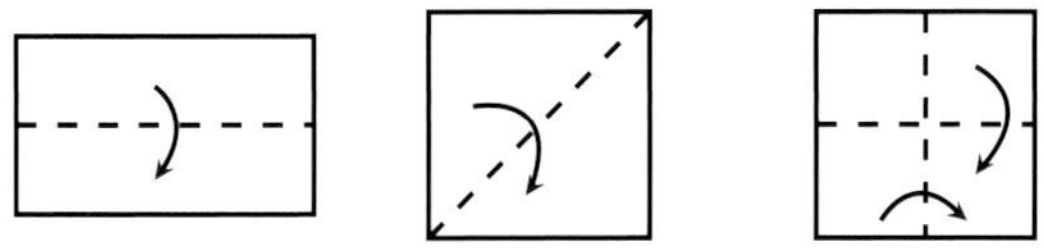

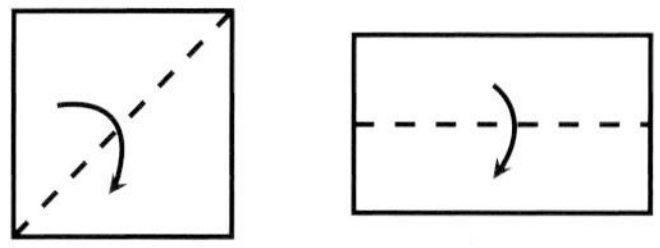

Make: 1   2   2

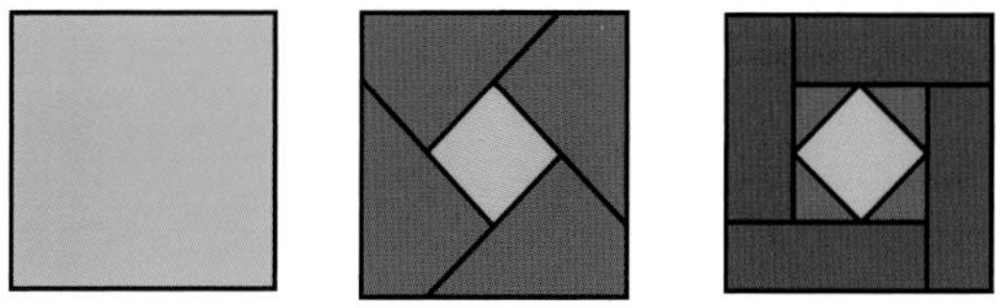

Step: 1   2   3

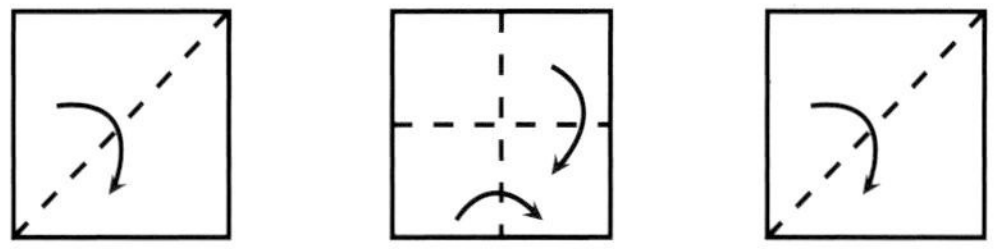

Step: 1   2   3

Make: 4   4   4

Make: 4   4   4

Step: 5   6   7

Step: 4   5   6

Stashbuster

CONSTRUCTION

Folded blocks

Follow the folding diagrams to make the 30 blocks.

ASSEMBLY

Lay out the blocks, sashing, and cornerstones as shown. Joint the components into rows. Join the rows.

Oregon Trail	Mosaic	Indian Meadows	Ohio Star	Saint Gregory's Cross
Double Wrench	Winged Four-Patch*	Friendship Chain	Hourglass	Framed Nine-Patch
Block in a Block	Canadian Gardens	Colonial Pavement	Ribbon Quilt Block	Twin Darts*
Card Basket	Mosaic Rose	Four-Star Fox & Goose	Weather-vane	Eight-Pointed Star
Old Maid's Puzzle	Puss in the Corner	Toad in the Puddle	Grand-mother's Choice	Ohio Star Variation
Tippe-canoe & Tyler Too	Card Trick*	Shoo Fly	Old Favorite	No Name

* Step 1 square does not show in finished block, so fabric choice doesn't matter.

Add the side and then the top and bottom borders, trimming the 2" x 31" strips to size.

FINISHING

Layer, add the split sleeve, and bind.

Scrap Happy

This is another sampler whose blocks are made entirely from leftover yardage, but the scraps are organized so that shapes within the blocks, such as the arrows in the Arrows block, are each made from the same fabric. We have been calling this "organized scrappy." To do this, you will need to reserve the larger pieces of fabric in your scrap selection for the blocks that use a fabric more than once.

SCRAP HAPPY, 18¾" x 28", MADE BY THE AUTHORS

Scrap Happy

The thirteen blocks range from simple to difficult, and the organized scrappy fabric layout makes it quite challenging. The fabric choices are based on value (light, medium, dark) more than on color, so if your scraps represent your stash, you might find out that you are missing a value and need to do a scrap swap with a friend.

Although this is a challenging sampler, using yardage rather than scraps would make this an intermediate project, since construction of the quilt, once the blocks are made, is simple.

MATERIALS

Fabric requirements

Yardage is based on fabric at least 40" wide and indicates only how much fabric was actually used, not the size of the scrap collection from which the fabrics were selected. Working from scraps, you will need more than this, but how much depends on the size of your scraps and whether you want to use the same fabric in more than one block.

Yardage or assorted scraps of the following:
34"	Lights (cream, white, very pale pastels, etc.)
13"	Medium-lights (stronger pastels, soft yellow, etc.)
24"	Mediums (red, rich pink, rust, soft green and blue, etc.)
25"	Darks (burgundy, forest green, navy, dark chocolate, etc.)
51"	black
4"	red (border)

Additional supplies

Batting: 22" x 33"
Metallic quilting thread (we used multicolor)

CUTTING DIRECTIONS

Sashing, backing, split sleeve, borders, and binding

From the black, cut:
Sashing:
10	1¼" x 4½"
4	2⅝" x 4½"
4	1¼" x 23½"
2	1¼" x 15½"

Border:
2	2½" x 18"
2	2½" x 25"

Binding:
2	1¼" x 21"
2	1¼" x 31"

Backing and split sleeve:
1	20" x 30"
2	11" x 6"

From the red, cut:
2 borders	¾" x 25"
2 borders	¾" x 16"

Folded blocks

The color chart below provides only the value needed for each step, and the photo of the sample shows when you need to use the same fabric more than once within a block. After sorting your scraps into lights, medium-lights, mediums, and darks, start pulling fabrics for each block, keeping in mind that Step 1 is always a 4½" square, and that Steps 2 and 3 will need more fabric than Steps 5 and 6. Check to make sure that there is enough to cut the block's components, replacing the too-small scraps with something similar.

For the blocks marked with an * on the assembly diagram (page 81), the basic square is covered up and never seen again, so if you have a limited supply of a certain fabric, you can substitute another fabric for your basic square in those blocks without affecting the final look.

See page 47 for the Sparkling Skies cutting chart and folding diagram.

Cut the components for 1 of each of these blocks.

See page 47 for the Sparkling Skies cutting chart and folding diagram.

CONSTRUCTION

Folded blocks

Follow the folding diagrams to make the blocks.

Block	Step 1	Step 2	Step 3	Step 4	Step 5	Step 6	Step 7
Dutch Pinwheel	Medium	Dark	Light	Medium-light	Medium		
Arrows	Light	Medium	Light	Medium	Medium	Dark	
Cups & Saucers	Medium	Light	Dark	Light	Dark	Light	Dark
Night & Day	Light	2 Medium & 2 Dark	2 Light & 2 Medium	2 Medium & 2 dark	2 Light & 2 Medium	2 light & 2 medium	
Friendship Square	Light	Dark	Light	Dark	Medium		
Twelve Triangles	Light	2 Light & 2 Dark	2 Light & 2 Dark	Medium			
Everybody's Favorite	Medium	Medium-light	Dark	Light	Light	Medium-light	
Cock's Comb	Medium	2 Medium & 2 Dark	Light	2 Medium & 2 dark	Medium	Light	
Gentleman's Fancy	Dark	Light	Medium-light	Dark	Light	Light	
Sparkling Skies	Medium	Dark	Dark	Light	Light	Medium	Medium
Birds in the Air	Light	Medium	Light	Medium	Light		
Beacon Lights	Dark	Light	Dark	Medium	Light	Dark	
Friendship Star	Dark	Light	Medium				

Dutch Pinwheel-easy

Step	Color	# of Pcs	Size	Folding Code
1	C	1	4½" x 4½"	-
2	E	4	3¼" x 4½"	D
3	A	4	3¼" x 3¼"	C
4	C	4	2" x 4½"	D
5	B	4	2" x 2"	B

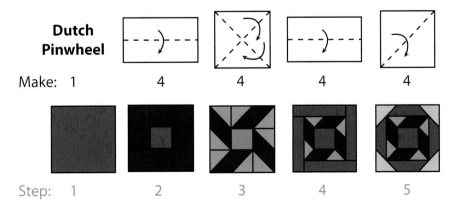

Dutch Pinwheel

Make: 1   4   4   4   4

Step: 1   2   3   4   5

Scrap Happy

Arrows-intermediate

Step	Color	# of Pcs	Size	Folding Code
1	A	1	4½" x 4½"	-
2	B, C, D, E	1 ea	4" x 4"	B
3	A	4	3½" x 3½"	C
4	B, C, D, E	1 ea	1½" x 3½"	E
5	B, C, D, E	1 ea	1½" x 3½"	E
6	B, C, D, E	1 ea	1½" x 1½"	A

Cups & Saucers-advanced

Step	Color	# of Pcs	Size	Folding Code
1	C	1	4½" x 4½"	-
2	A	4	3¼" x 4½"	D
3	D, E	2 ea	3¼" x 3¼"	B
4	A	4	1⅞" x 4½"	D
5	D, E	2 ea	2½" x 2½"	B
6	B	4	2" x 2"	B
7	D, E	2 ea	1¼" x 1¼"	B

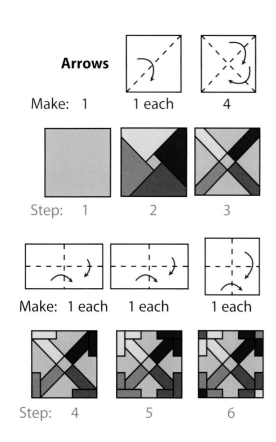

Arrows

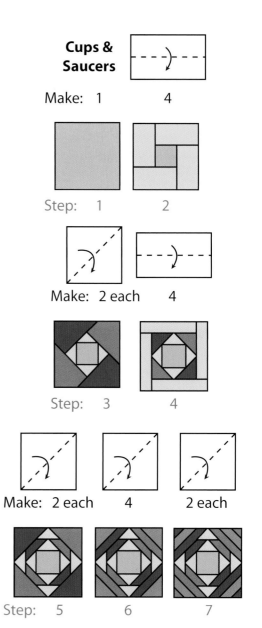

Cups & Saucers

Night & Day-intermediate

Step	Color	# of Pcs	Size	Folding Code
1	A	1	4½" x 4½"	-
2	B, C, D, E	1 ea	4½" x 4½"	A
3	A, B, C, D	1 ea	3½" x 3½"	A
4	B, C, D, E	1 ea	2½" x 2½"	B
5	A, B, C, D	1 ea	1½" x 2½"	G-2
6	A, B, C, D	1 ea	1½" x 2½"	G-1

Friendship Square-easy

Step	Color	# of Pcs	Size	Folding Code
1	A	1	4½" x 4½"	-
2	B, C, D, E	1 ea	4½" x 4½"	A
3	A	4	3¼" x 3¼"	B
4	B, C, D, E	1 ea	2½" x 2½"	B
5	B, C, D, E	1 ea	2½" x 2½"	A

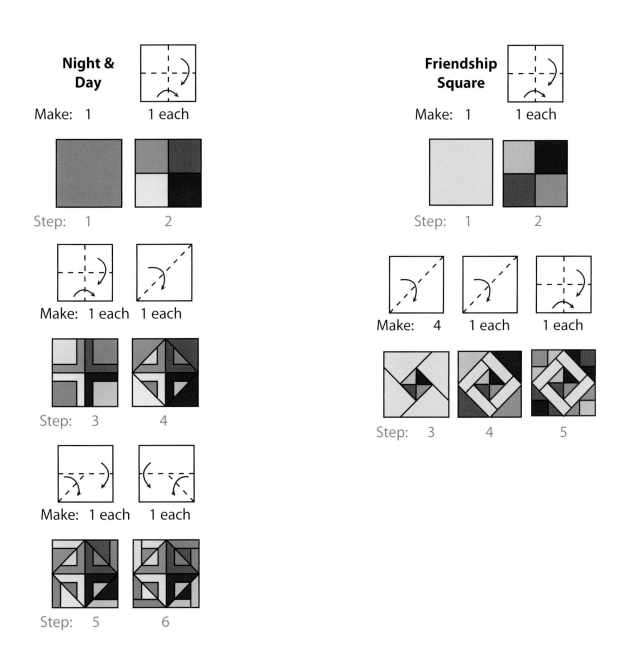

Scrap Happy

Twelve Triangles-easy

Step	Color	# of Pcs	Size	Folding Code
1	A	1	4½" x 4½"	-
2	A, B, C, D	1 ea	4½" x 4½"	C
3	A, B, C, D	1 ea	2½" x 4½"	D
4	B, C, D, E	1 ea	2½" x 2½"	B

Everybody's Favorite-intermediate

Step	Color	# of Pcs	Size	Folding Code
1	C	1	4½" x 4½"	-
2	B	4	4" x 4"	B
3	D	4	3½" x 3½"	C
4	A	4	2½" x 3½"	E
5	A	4	2½" x 3½"	E
6	C	4	2½" x 2½"	A

Twelve Triangles

Make: 1   1 each

Step: 1   2

Make: 1 each   1 each

Step: 3   4

Everybody's Favorite

Make: 1   4

Step: 1   2

Make: 4   4

Step: 3   4

Make: 4   4

Step: 5   6

Cock's Comb-intermediate

Step	Color	# of Pcs	Size	Folding Code
1	B	1	4½" x 4½"	-
2	B, E	2 ea	2¾" x 4½"	I
3	A, C	4 ea	3½" x 3½"	C
4	B, D	2 ea	2½" x 4½"	D
5	C	4	2½" x 2½"	C
6	A	4	2½" x 2½"	C

Gentleman's Fancy-intermediate

Step	Color	# of Pcs	Size	Folding Code
1	D	1	4½" x 4½"	-
2	A	4	3¼" x 4½"	D
3	C	4	3¼" x 3¼"	B
4	E	4	1⅞" x 4½"	D
5	A	4	1⅞" x 1⅞"	C
6	B	4	2" x 2"	B

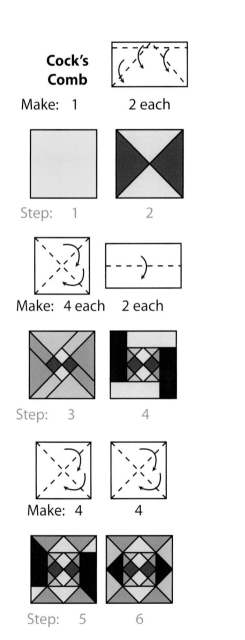

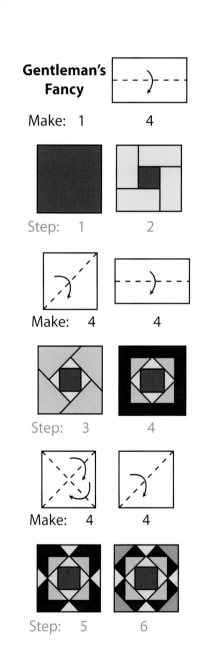

Scrap Happy

Birds in the Air-easy

Step	Color	# of Pcs	Size	Folding Code
1	A	1	4½" x 4½"	-
2	B, C, D, E	1 ea	4½" x 4½"	A
3	A	4	2½" x 2½"	B
4	B, C, D, E	1 ea	2½" x 2½"	A
5	A	4	1½" x 1½"	B

Beacon Lights-intermediate

Step	Color	# of Pcs	Size	Folding Code
1	D	1	4½" x 4½"	-
2	B	4	3½" x 3½"	B
3	D	4	2½" x 2½"	B
4	C	4	2½" x 2½"	C
5	A	8	1½" x 1½"	C
6	A	4	2½" x 2½"	A

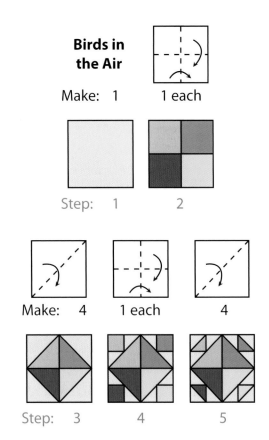

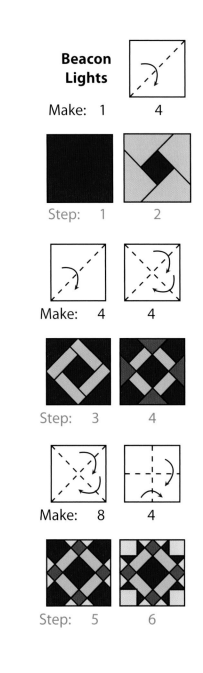

Friendship Star-easy

Step	Color	# of Pcs	Size	Folding Code
1	D	1	4½" x 4½"	-
2	A	4	3¼" x 4½"	D
3	C	4	3¼" x 3¼"	G-2

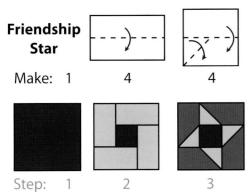

Friendship Star

Make: 1   4   4

Step: 1   2   3

ASSEMBLY

Lay out the components as shown and join them in vertical rows. Join the rows.

Borders

Add the narrow red border and the final outer border.

FINISHING YOUR QUILT

Layer, quilt, add the split sleeve, and bind.

The sample is quilted very lightly with metallic thread, just an outline in the 4 black corner rectangles and on either side of the red border. The binding was sewn on from the back (with regular thread), folded over to the front and topstitched with the same metallic thread used for quilting.

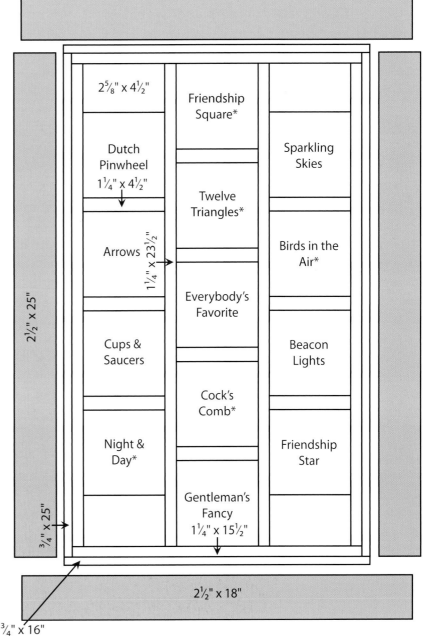

* Step 1 square does not show in finished block.

Measuring borders for projects without quilted areas

When measuring for borders, the general practice is to measure across the center length and width of a quilt, since the outer raw edges tend to stretch from handling. For projects with quilted areas, such as FLANDERS FIELDS, this is what we recommend. However, for projects where the quilt top is border-to-border blocks, such as STASHBUSTER, it would not be possible to ease any more than the slightest bit of extra length. Therefore, just measure the outer lengths and widths and average those.

Adding borders to folded-block sashing

To add a border onto the sashing or narrow border beside a folded block, it is easiest to sew them on with the back of the quilt top facing up and the border on the feed dogs. When sewing borders to the narrow sashing, there simply isn't enough room for the presser foot to sit beside the block. With the blocks on the bottom, the foot will tend to slip off the block. If you sew with the border on the bottom, the foot can slip slightly under or between the layers of the block, making it easier to keep to a ¼" seam allowance.

For quilts with wide borders or spaces that require quilting

Depending on your batting thickness and the thickness of your blocks, you may want to use an extra layer of batting in the border area to bring the height of the quilted area up level with the folded blocks.

Lay your quilt top right-side down on your work surface and center batting on top. Pin lightly into position. Locate the folded blocks under the batting, and draw an outline around the blocks to indicate where to cut. Then cut the batting away from behind the blocks, taking care not to cut into your quilt top. You can remove the batting from the quilt top to cut it, but then reposition, and pin lightly once more to hold it in place when you flip it over. Turn it right-side up, re-pin the batting, and remove the pins from the back. Tape your backing onto your work surface so that it is wrinkle free. Place the batting and quilt top onto the backing and pin. Quilt as desired. Trim the backing and batting even and square your quilt. Add sleeves and bind.

If your quilt top does not have wide borders or spaces that require quilting

Batting is optional for quilts with only folded blocks and no borders at all. However, batting provides a layer of protection when you are hand stitching the lower edge of the sleeve onto the backing, ensuring that you don't stitch into the quilt top. If you choose not to include batting in a project make sure your backing fabric is as light as the basic square fabric so that it doesn't show through.

Tape your backing onto your work surface so that it is wrinkle free. Place the batting and quilt top onto backing and pin. Trim the backing and batting even and square your quilt. Add sleeves and bind.

Split sleeve

Our preference, especially for smaller quilts, is to make a split sleeve, one that allows a quilt to be hung with a threaded eyehook and dowel on a single nail when a more decorative method isn't available or desired.

Measure the top of your quilt (for example, 20"), and divide that number by 2 (10"). Then cut two rectangles 6" by that half measurement (6" x 10"). Fold under ½" along all of the 6" edges and sew in place. Fold the rectangle in half along the length, and press.

Line up the raw edges of both sleeves at the top back edge of your quilt so that the ends are about ⅜" to ½" from the sides (to leave room for the binding) and pin in place.

After you have bound your quilt, slip stitch or blind stitch the folded edge of the sleeves to the back of the quilt.

Sleeve for a point-ended quilt

To make the sleeve, cut a square of fabric with a diagonal measurement equal to the widest part of the quilt. Fold the square in half diagonally, and press. Fold the points opposite the pressed fold to the inside of the triangle about 1½" and press. Topstitch if desired. Place the sleeve at the top on the back of the quilt, aligning the raw edges. Pin in place and bind your quilt.

Triangular hanger

Here is a simple and economical solution for hanging narrow quilts with triangular ends, such as the BREEZE CATCHER and GEMSTONES. It would probably work for larger quilts as well, with different materials, of course.

Take the lid of a one gallon ice cream pail or margarine tub, and cut the edge off with a sturdy pair of scissors. Draw and cut a square with a diagonal measurement ¼" bigger than the base of your sleeve, and remove a thin strip diagonally across the center, leaving yourself with two right-angle triangles.

Make a hole at the top of each triangle using a hole punch, making sure that the holes are centered and that they line up when the triangles are back to back. (If necessary, trim the triangles so that this is the case.) Slip both triangles inside the sleeve so that the hole peeks over the top edge of the sleeve, and use this to attach a piece of string, ribbon, or chain for hanging.

You can, of course, make a triangle from a thin piece of wood or Plexiglas®, but the stiffness of two layers of plastic is sufficient to keep a small quilt from sagging.

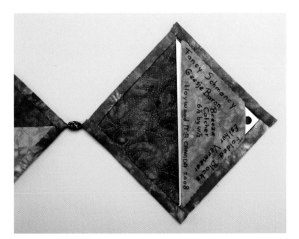

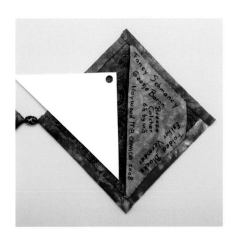

Single-layer binding with butted corners

With the back of the quilt facing up, pin binding strips along the top and bottom edges of the quilt, right sides together. Stitch with ¼" seam allowance. Trim the ends of the strips even with the sides of the quilt.

Wrap the binding over to the front of the quilt, and tuck the raw edges under so that they just cover the ¼" stitching line. Pin in place. Using a thread that matches the binding or the same thread used in quilting, topstitch in place. Stitch the remaining two strips to the sides of the quilt and fold in the ends. Then fold the binding strips to the front and topstitch.

Alternatively, you can sew the binding to the front, fold over to the back, and secure with a blind stitch or slip stitch.

Double-fold binding

The varying thicknesses of the blocks make it challenging to regulate the width of a double-fold binding, so we recommend its use only for those who wish to hand finish their binding to the backs of their quilts.

Measure the circumference of your quilt, add 5", and cut a 2¼" strip this length, piecing the strip if necessary. Fold the strip in half lengthwise with wrong sides together and press.

Leaving 3" of the end of the strip free, start sewing the binding to the front of the quilt at least 2" before a corner. Stop stitching ¼" from the corner.

The miter

Fold the binding away from the quilt at a 90-degree angle to the line of stitching so that there is a diagonal fold in the binding, then fold the binding back along the next side of the quilt, aligning the straight fold with the raw edge of the side just sewn and aligning the raw edges of the binding with the next side to be sewn. Secure the corner and start stitching ¼" from the edge. Sew to the next corner and repeat the folding steps at the corners. Stop stitching 4" before the starting point.

Loose ends

Once you have sewn around the quilt, unfold both ends of your binding and cut them on the same diagonal, making sure the "beginning" and "end" will overlap an inch or slightly more. Fold over and press a generous ¼" into the end to create a finished edge, and refold. Then lay the beginning on top of the end. Finish sewing the binding in place. Fold the binding to the back side of the quilt and secure with a blind stitch or slip stitch.

Depending on how much handling the binding will receive, you may wish to blind stitch the binding join as well.

BONUS BLOCKS

Fading Star-advanced

Step	Color	# of Pcs	Size	Folding Code
1	F	1	4½" x 4½"	-
2	A	4	3¼" x 4½"	D
3	F	4	3¼" x 3¼"	B
4	B	4	1⅞" x 1⅞"	C
5	E	4	3¼" x 3¼"	A
6	D	4	2¼" x 2¼"	A
7	C	4	1½" x 1½"	A

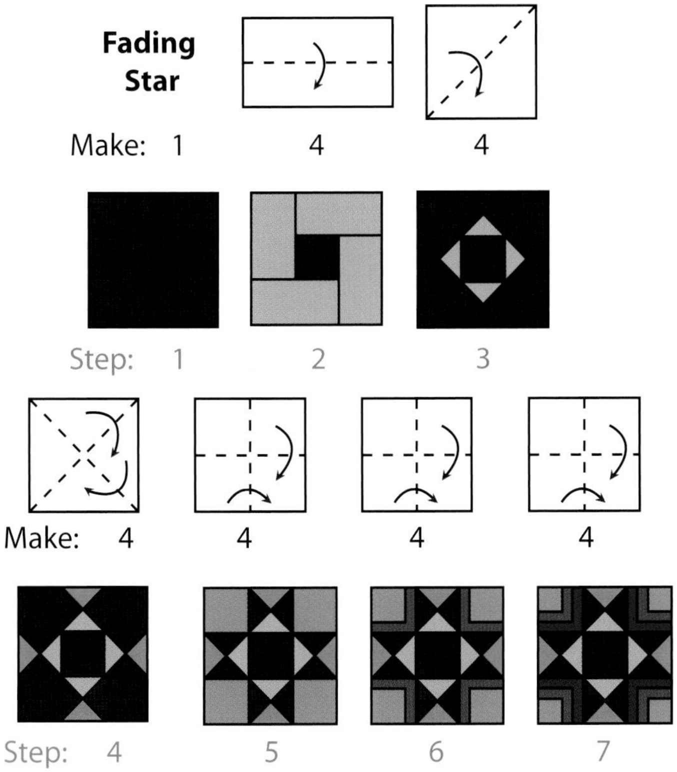

Framed Nine-Patch #2

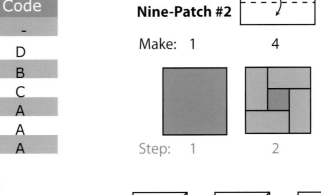

Fading Star

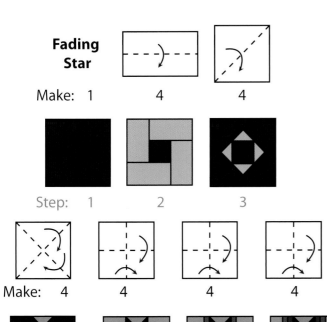

House-advanced

Step	Color	# of Pcs	Size	Folding Code
1	D	1	4½" x 4½"	-
2	C	1	4½" x 5¼"	D
3	B	2	1⅝" x 3¾"	F
4	C	1	2⅛" x 5¼"	E
5	A	2	2⅛" x 2⅛"	B
6	A	1	2⅛" x 4½"	D
7	E	2	1⅝" x 2⅛"	F

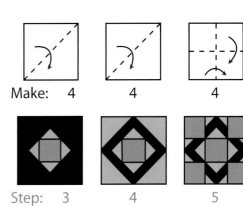

Framed Nine-Patch #2-easy

Step	Color	# of Pcs	Size	Folding Code
1	D	1	4½" x 4½"	-
2	A	4	3¼" x 4½"	D
3	E	4	3¼" x 3¼"	B
4	B	4	2¼" x 2¼"	B
5	C	4	3¼" x 3¼"	A

House

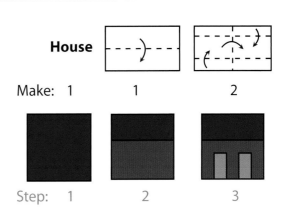

Bonus Blocks

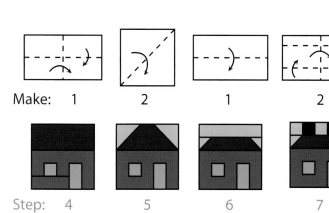

Make: 1 2 1 2

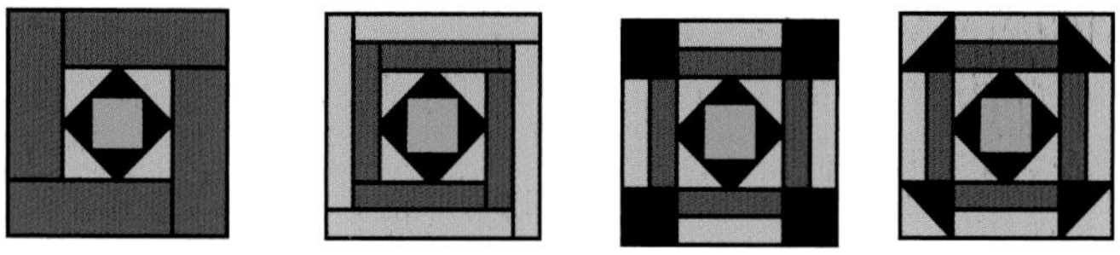

Step: 4 5 6 7

Ruins of Jericho-advanced

Step	Color	# of Pcs	Size	Folding Code
1	D	1	4½" x 4½"	-
2	A	4	3½" x 3½"	B
3	C	4	2½" x 4½"	D
4	B	4	1½" x 2½"	F
5	A	4	1½" x 4½"	D
6	D	4	2½" x 2½"	A
7	A	4	1½" x 1½"	B

Magic Box-advanced

Step	Color	# of Pcs	Size	Folding Code
1	C	1	4½" x 4½"	-
2	E	4	3¾" x 4½"	D
3	B	4	3¾" x 3¾"	B
4	C	4	3" x 4½"	D
5	A	4	1¾" x 4½"	D
6	E	4	3" x 3"	A
7	A	4	1¾" x 1¾"	B

Ruins of Jericho

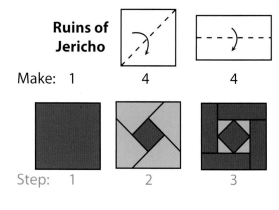

Make: 1 4 4

Step: 1 2 3

Magic Box

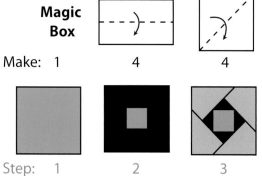

Make: 1 4 4

Step: 1 2 3

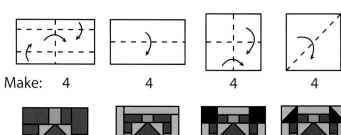

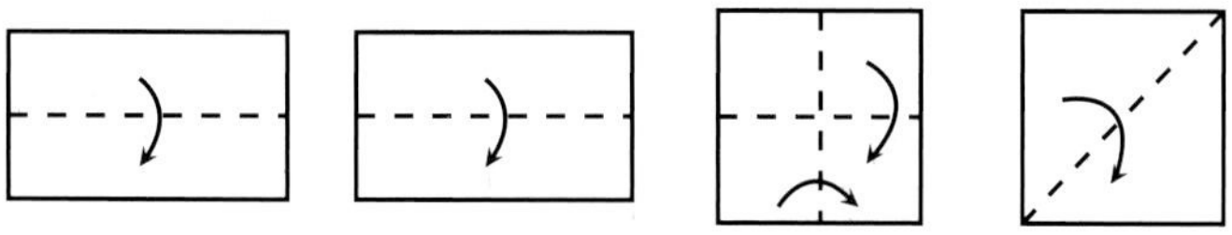

Make: 4 4 4 4

Step: 4 5 6 7

The House That Jack Built-intermediate

Step	Color	# of Pcs	Size	Folding Code
1	B	1	4½" x 4½"	-
2	C	4	3½" x 3½"	B
3	D	4	2¾" x 2¾"	B
4	E	4	2" x 2"	B
5	F	4	1¼" x 1¼"	B
6	A	4	2½" x 2 ½"	C

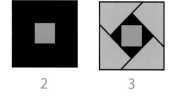

Make: 4 4 4 4

Step: 4 5 6 7

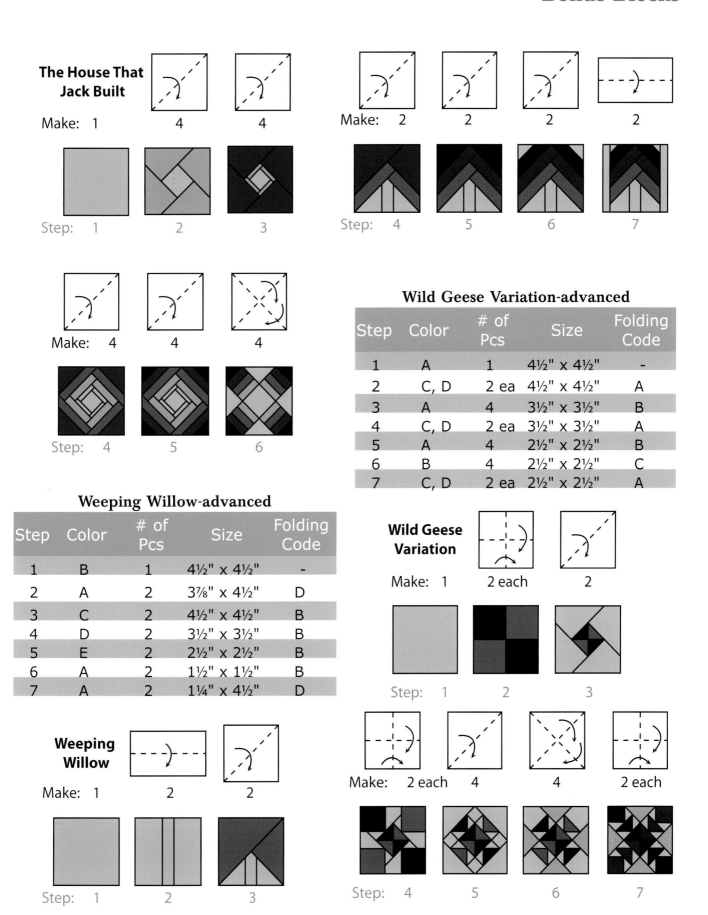

The House That Jack Built

Make: 1   4   4

Step: 1   2   3

Make: 2   2   2   2

Step: 4   5   6   7

Make: 4   4   4

Step: 4   5   6

Wild Geese Variation-advanced

Step	Color	# of Pcs	Size	Folding Code
1	A	1	4½" x 4½"	-
2	C, D	2 ea	4½" x 4½"	A
3	A	4	3½" x 3½"	B
4	C, D	2 ea	3½" x 3½"	A
5	A	4	2½" x 2½"	B
6	B	4	2½" x 2½"	C
7	C, D	2 ea	2½" x 2½"	A

Weeping Willow-advanced

Step	Color	# of Pcs	Size	Folding Code
1	B	1	4½" x 4½"	-
2	A	2	3⅞" x 4½"	D
3	C	2	4½" x 4½"	B
4	D	2	3½" x 3½"	B
5	E	2	2½" x 2½"	B
6	A	2	1½" x 1½"	B
7	A	2	1¼" x 4½"	D

Wild Geese Variation

Make: 1   2 each   2

Step: 1   2   3

Weeping Willow

Make: 1   2   2

Step: 1   2   3

Make: 2 each   4   4   2 each

Step: 4   5   6   7

**FANCY SCHMANCY FOLDED BLOCKS,
MADE BY GEESJE BARON**

Canadian Gardens p. 40

Dutch Pinwheel p. 75

Cock's Comb p. 79

Double Wrench p. 61

Framed Nine-Patch p. 62

Night & Day p. 77

Eight-Pointed Star p. 66

Duck Tracks p. 26

Friendship Chain p. 62

Oregon Trail p. 52

Aunt Dinah p. 19

Twin Darts p. 64

No Name p. 71

Philidelphia Pavements p. 53

Card Basket p. 65

Union Squares p. 14

Ribbon Quilt Block p. 64

Poppy Block p. 27

Magic Box p. 86

Framed Nine-Patch #2 p. 85

Ohio Star Variation p. 51

No Name p. 71

Log Cabin Variation p. 55

Arrows p. 76

Fading Star p. 85

Ohio Star p. 60

Friendship Square p. 77

Puss in the Corner p. 67

Mosaic Rose p. 65

Friendship Star p. 81

The House That Jack Built p. 86-87

Ruins of Jericho p. 86

Salt Lake City p. 52

Sandhills p. 29-30

Northumberland Star p. 45 & 51

Grand-mother's Choice p. 68

Wild Geese Variation p. 87

Soldier's Cross p. 41

Fool's Square p. 48

Sparkling Skies p. 47

Four-Star Fox & Goose p. 46

Old Favorite p. 70

House p. 85

Missouri Star p. 51

State of Illinois p. 53

Saint Gregory's Cross p. 45

Twelve Triangles p. 78

Colonial Pavement p. 63

Old Maid's Puzzle p. 67

Log Cabin Variation p. 55

Mrs. Keller's Nine-Patch p. 46

Weather-vane p. 66

Cups & Saucers p. 76

Leaf Block p. 40

Indian Meadows p. 60

Shoo Fly p. 70

Fading Star p. 85

Everybody's Favorite p. 78

Indiana Puzzle p. 13

Weeping Willow p. 87

Gentleman's Fancy p. 79

Mosaic p. 33-34

Card Trick p. 69

Woodbox p. 23

Beacon Lights p. 80

Winged Four-Patch p. 33-34

Star & Square p. 47

Toad in the Puddle p. 68

Dutch City p. 14

Birds in the Air p. 80

Block in a Block p. 63

FOLDING METHODS

Press after each fold.

FOLDING METHOD A
Fold a square in half and in half again to
form a quarter-size square with 2 finished
(folded) sides.

Symbol   Folding Steps

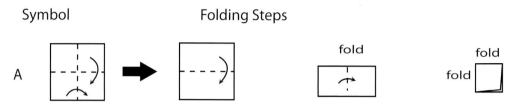

OPTIONAL FOLDING METHOD A
Fold a square in half on the diagonal. Fold
in the corners along the fold to meet the
third corner, forming a quarter-size square
with the folded edges in the center.

FOLDING METHOD B
Fold a square in half once on the diagonal.

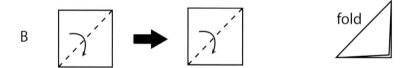

FOLDING METHOD C
Fold a square in half on the diagonal and
fold again on the diagonal to form a quarter-
size triangle.

FOLDING METHOD D
Fold a rectangle in half lengthwise.

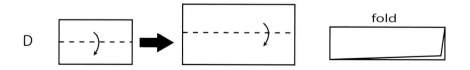

FOLDING METHOD E

Fold a rectangle in half lengthwise, then fold in half again across the width.

FOLDING METHOD F

Fold in the 2 long edges of a rectangle so that they meet in the center, making a long thin strip. Fold the strip in half across the width to form a rectangle with 3 finished sides.

FOLDING METHOD G1

Fold a square in half, and then fold the right corner over, lining up the raw edges as shown.

FOLDING METHOD G2

Fold a square in half, and then fold the left corner over, aligning the raw edges as shown.

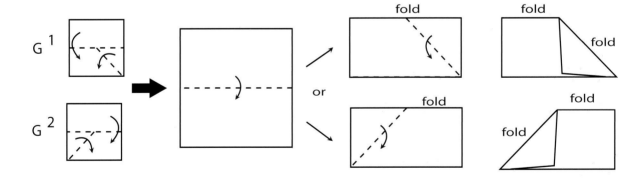

Folding Methods

FOLDING METHOD H

Fold a rectangle in half lengthwise, then fold in both corners, aligning the raw edges.

Symbol   Folding Steps

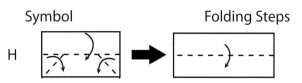

FOLDING METHOD I

Fold over one long edge of a rectangle ½", then fold in both corners so that the folded edge meets in the middle to form a triangle with 2 finished edges.

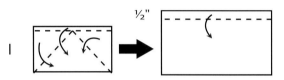

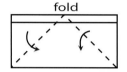

FOLDING METHOD J

Fold over one long edge of a rectangle ½", then fold both corners in so that the folded edge does not quite meet in the middle. Fold in half to form a triangle with 2 finished edges with the folded edges on the inside.

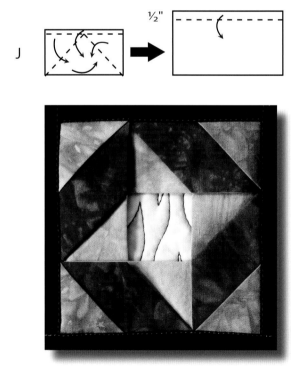

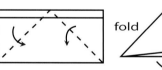

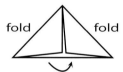

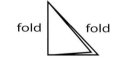

Authors photos by Miranda Hardern

ESTHER VERMEER

GEESJE BARON

After car-pooling to guild meetings together for about five years, we realized that summer was too long a season to put the quilting supplies away, so we started meeting weekly to quilt together year round. It wasn't long before we began talking about writing a book.

About the Authors

Our book is a complete collaboration, a pooling of the ideas and abilities of two quilters. Aside from the two little biographies below, it is written in first person plural, "Weeeeeeeeee!"

Something about Geesje:

I'll start by telling you that my name is pronounced "Gay-shuh" and I am the co-owner/operator of a dairy farm an hour west of Winnipeg, Manitoba. Over the last 26 years, I have raised four boys and milked sixty cows, together with my husband, all the while taking classes in weaving, spinning, quilting, and fabric painting.

I began learning how to quilt in 1986, took my first quilting class in 1989, and joined Klokkequiltsters (Wijnewoude, The Netherlands) in 1992, which was where I first learned about folded blocks.

After immigrating to Canada in 1995, I founded the Morning Glory Quilters in Carman, Manitoba, together with Joan Vandersluis, and began teaching classes in 1999 through the Golden Prairie Arts Council. I enjoy the challenge of making new patterns and passing on tips and tricks to students on a variety of subjects, including folded blocks, stained glass quilting, Seminole piecing, quilted clothing construction, and other topics. I also teach workshops for our two local guilds.

In 2004, I entered two quilts in a provincial juried art show for the first time. SPIDER'S WEB in MORNING DEW won for my category, and went on to hang in the Manitoba Legislative Building. I was next honored with a one-woman quilt show in Carman in November and December of 2006. In addition to designing quilts for my own home, I have sold commissioned quilts, quilt patterns, and finished quilts including a very complex original design, GALLERY OF QUILTS, that used Katie Pasquini Masopust's techniques for dimensional piecework.

Most recently, I entered KNOT IN FLOW MOTION, a Log Cabin quilt depicting a Celtic-like design, in the 2009 Canadian Quilters' Association National Juried Show and won an Honorable Mention rosette! I currently do custom machine quilting on my mid-arm and domestic sewing machines, and have developed a Web site together with my youngest son to market custom-dyed and painted fabric (www.conundrumquilts.com).

Now a bit about Esther:

Like Geesje, I am a Dutch immigrant. However, I came to Canada just a few days before starting kindergarten in 1972. My earliest memories are of coloring while lying on the floor with my mother, learning to stitch and knot, and making sketch after sketch of animals, favorite rock stars, old apple trees, or whatever caught my eye, all drawn onto any bit of paper I could get my hands on.

At the age of eleven, my aunt took me to a sewing shop and bought some pretty black corduroy with little houses on it. I started sewing then and eventually began designing my own clothes. At one of my first jobs in a daycare, I painted murals on every bare wall I could find. Yet, although my heart was in the arts, a practical streak eventually turned my head toward earning a degree in the sciences, during and after which I worked as a landscaper, lab instructor, researcher, and consultant.

Eventually, my sweetheart and I bought a small farm in rural Manitoba, about a mile away from Geesje's farm. She and I met in 2000, at the Haywood Country Store, and became instant friends. That fall, I joined her at the Morning Glory Quilters meetings, and later, the Material Girls Quilting Guild. I quickly discovered a new passion for my sewing machine between running after 300 free-range chickens, mowing acres of grass, and changing diapers.

Now, as the work-from-home mother of two little girls, I design and make quilts, teach workshops on folded blocks, color theory, quilt embellishing, and other topics. I also give painting and quilting lessons in my home studio and just finished my third year of writing the monthly newsletter for the Morning Glory Quilters (www.esthervermeer.com).

BIBLIOGRAPHY AND RESOURCES

Noordhuis, Liesbeth. *Vouw Patchwork (Folding Patchwork).* Maestro-Hobby, The Netherlands, 1995.

Cedar Canyon Textiles, Inc. The Paintstik® Place
http://www.cedarcanyontextiles.com/learning.php
Their learning center has all kinds of information about using Shiva® Artist's Paintstiks.

http://www.3dfoldedblocks.com

http://www.quilterscache.com

http://www.quilttownusa.com/mom/3dpatchworkbeginners.htm

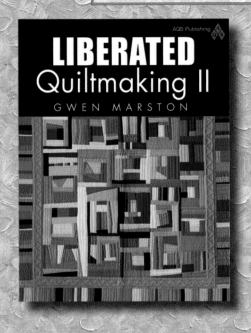

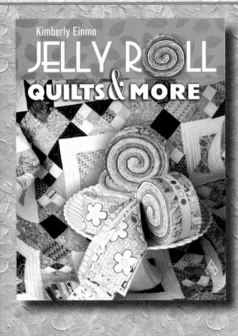
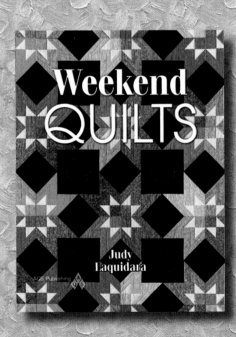